Mosaics of

FISHBOURNE ROMAN PALACE

by **Derrick Napier**

First published in Great Britain as a softback original in 2015

Typeset in Century Schoolbook

Editing, design and publishing by UK Book Publishing

UK Book Publishing is a trading name of Consilience Media

www.ukbookpublishing.com

ISBN: 978-1-910223-21-5

Contents

Overview
Fishbourne Roman Palace

The emergence of Fishbourne lies within its physical environment as three streams which flow from the north to the south eventually converge to form the head of Fishbourne Harbour. Sir Barry Cunliffe, in 'Volume 1 (The Site) of The 1960s Excavations at Fishbourne', explains in detail what the local environment was like at the time of the Roman conquest. He explains how the joint force of water from the issuing streams, from the south and from the east, was sufficient to scour the eastern creek-end which prevented silt accumulating in the main channel. This in turn allowed a sufficient depth of water to give shipping a safe passage to sail close to the shore. The western creek-end had two streams, one flowing from the north and the other from the west. These converged to form a wide and safe inlet. At the north eastern extremity of the Fishbourne inlet was a natural lagoon-shaped harbour and, therefore, this was a major attraction and asset for any invading seafaring forces.

This then was the lush and varied scene which greeted Roman eyes as the occupation of Britannia began in AD 43. Upon their arrival the archaeology suggests that the open area to the east of the present Roman Palace was utilised initially as a military supply-base. Timber harbour warehouses were seemingly constructed, although the main military base for the troops probably lies somewhere within Chichester. When the Roman army, possibly the Legio II Augusta, under the command of Vaspasian, moved on, the military supply-base buildings were replaced by a commercial development. No doubt, merchants and smaller traders would have utilised the 'modern' harbour construction and the Roman road grid system for their financial benefits. During the reign of Vaspasian, about AD 73, to enable the construction of the Flavian Palace, the stream running through the proposed site was diverted slightly to the east and the original valley was filled with clay and gravel to provide a dry and solid platform for its foundations. Prior to the rise of the Flavian Roman Palace, an earlier luxurious masonry building, the Proto-Palace, was built about AD 60 during the reign of Nero. Much of this building was incorporated into the south east of the East Wing of the later Roman Palace.

Chapter I

THE DISCOVERY (RUINS, ROTAS AND ROMANCES)

Easter of 1961 was, in all probability, at least to most of us, no different from any other previous Easter. But to a small gathering of students and archaeologists assembled in a farmer's field in Fishbourne, it would turn out to be an Easter that would be rooted in their memories for the rest of their lives.

In my mind's eye I can see them now: a group of young and vibrant people with some of the young men already sporting long hair and newly grown beards. A few of the students will be in possession, in their back pockets, of shiny, virgin trowels. While others will be discreetly cleaning theirs of the remnants of the last time they were used.

What was the weather like that morning of the first day? Well, if it was dry and bright or dull and cloudy, or even a little damp, it would have had little effect on the atmosphere. The atmosphere of expectancy must have been highly charged, no doubt fuelled by Barry Cunliffe and Margaret Rule, the archaeologists in charge of the excavations, telling them about the archaeology which had been seen, identified and rescued from the trench carved out by the local Water Board in April of the previous year. Then it would have begun – the opening chapter of the remarkable story of the discovery of Fishbourne Roman Palace.

The excavations lasted from 1961-1968, with a short excavation to the south of the site in 1969 ending on the 28th March that year. A model of how the Palace may have looked in the late first century AD was commissioned, and Thorpes, the model builders in Norwich, took up the challenge. The model is still on display in the foyer of the Palace entrance. The site was officially opened to the public on Tuesday 28th May 1968 by the Bishop of Chichester.

The excavations over those years attracted a vast group of people: students of archaeology, older experienced excavators and many volunteers. Some would attend short-term, or whenever possible - others regularly, even over the whole seven seasons of excavations. Who were these people? Where were they from? What were their daily thoughts and emotions – as mosaic after mosaic loomed up before their eyes? When the excavations were concluded, where did their lives take them and what were their memories of their time spent in helping to resurrect the Roman Palace?

Suddenly, an opportunity arose to find answers to all those questions. For early in 2010 a reorganisation and refurbishment of the main offices at Fishbourne unearthed archives, some relating to the original excavations. The then director, Christine Medlock, asked the North Wing staff if they would be willing to look through the archive material to see whether there was enough interesting material on which to base an exhibition to celebrate the 50th anniversary of the discovery of the Palace's remains.

All the archive material was relocated to the Research Room in the Collections and Discovery Centre and Sheila Marsden, a Senior Museum Assistant, kindly invited me to join the North Wing staff – Anne-Marie Williams, Sylvia Arnold, Tess Fradgeley, Julie Harrington and Jan Christie – to help view the reams of photographs, articles, letters and correspondence, to filter out any relating to the 1960s excavations.

It was agreed that we would all meet in the Research Room on Wednesdays to take an initial look at what had been discovered. Well, when I walked in to that room on the first Wednesday, there piled against the far wall was a collection of boxes, folders and photo albums. I felt like a small boy who had suddenly been left alone in a sweet shop. I resisted the surging temptation to touch and waited for the rest of the team to arrive.

Soon we were all together, all sat at the long table and apprehensively eyeing the volume of material that was before us. The atmosphere of apprehension was disturbed by a voice saying, 'Let's get on with a couple of hours of research then we can enjoy sandwiches and tea.' We all took a small pile of the archive; thus our journey back in time began.

At this point we had no idea what the exhibition would be about or what it would be called. But within that room there were seven minds combined together with a passion of resolve, each one full of determination that from within the reams of archive, we would conceive and give birth to an exhibition worthy of a public display and one, as individuals, we could be proud of.

The archive revealed itself to be an Aladdin's Cave of newspaper articles, photographs, correspondence and local residents' reactions and opinions, all related to the discovery and excavation of the Roman remains. As we continued to view the archive, what began to capture the team's interest and kindle our imaginations, was the discovery of such items as bills from local tradesmen regarding food and other essentials vital to the day-to-day running of the site. There was also correspondence regarding the organisation of accommodation for the volunteers, and all seemed to be the responsibility of Mrs Margaret Rule.

As the flood of information from the archive started to recede, our ideas began to find firmer ground on what the exhibition would be about. The decision was made: it would be focused on the life and experiences of the excavators who dug at Fishbourne between 1961 and 1969. The exhibition would conclude with information regarding the archaeological and academic achievements of some of the excavators after the conclusion of their time at Fishbourne.

After a long and fun-filled debate, it was agreed that the exhibition would carry the title of 'Ruins, Rotas and Romances'. Then the question arose of how we would present it and was there enough material to produce 18 boards? The boards (pictured below) would start in the museum and then continue down the North Wing wall, concluding with a display in the Lower Concourse – near where the discovery trench was ploughed in 1960.

Next to the discovery trench a dummy of an excavator, complete with wheelbarrow and excavating tools, was placed – a visual aid to promote the theme of the exhibition. A local radio station kindly gave us a regular five minute spot to promote the 50 years on anniversary and the Director and a team member engaged their thoughts with the listening public. The local papers and the magazine 'Current Archaeology' kindly found space in their publications to give the exhibition a mention.

The 18 boards were created by each team member being responsible for identifying the archive material relating to the title of the boards they were working on. Each board would carry, on the top left hand corner, a logo of a wheelbarrow and on some boards a timeline was created listing the world news headlines between the years 1960-68.

Then the exhibition gratefully received, from Mr Geoffrey Claridge, a copy of a cine-film he had recorded showing the day to day life on site of the excavators. This remarkable piece of archive material could be viewed on the computer just inside the entrance of the museum, and before the first board of the 'Ruins, Rotas and Romances' exhibition. The film can still be viewed in the museum.

The 18 boards carried the following titles (many with pictures):

RUINS, ROTAS AND ROMANCES

During recent office renovations at Fishbourne Roman Palace a bundle of paperwork was discovered, relating to the original excavations that had taken place at Fishbourne throughout the 1960s.

These excavations revealed the remains of the vast Roman building that you see beneath the cover building and beyond, and much has been written about the archaeology uncovered during these "digs".

However, the recently-found documents tell a different tale. They give an insight into how the excavations were run, how many volunteers were needed, how they were accommodated, and what they did while they were here.

This fascinating story has yet to be told, and it seemed appropriate this year, the 50th anniversary of the Palace's discovery, to tell all…

BENEFACTORS AND DIRECTORS I

We would not be here without the people below. Their hard work and dedication to the site made what you see today possible.

IVAN D MARGARY FSA

Ivan Margary, the Palace's benefactor, was born in 1896, the son of Colonel Alfred Robert and Lillian Margary. He died in 1976.

What the visitor views of the Palace here today is preserved because of the generosity and vision of this man. He purchased the site from the farmer, Mr Ledger, for £50,000 in 1963 when the land was threatened with a housing development. By the time the Palace was open to the public, at the end of May 1968, the Mr Margary had donated nearly £100,000 (equivalent to approximately £1.5 million today) to the project. He handed the site over to the Sussex Archaeological Society for safe keeping and a plaque recording this can be seen in the foyer.

More can be learned about his life and achievements at the end of the displays – further down the North Wing.

PROFESSOR SIR BARRY CUNLIFFE CBE

Barry Cunliffe was born on 10 December 1939. His archaeological appetite was whetted aged 9 on his uncle's farm, in Somerset, while escaping from bomb-scarred Portsmouth. Pitney Villa was a delight for him, as he frequently found tesserae and bits of Roman tile.

When aged 16, he excavated at Muntham Court with a Mr Holleyman and Mr Burstow, he became initiated into how sites were excavated in Sussex at that time.

He read Archaeology and Anthropolgy at Cambridge, gaining a First and in 1963 became a lecturer at Bristol University. In 1966 he became a Professor when taking the Chair at the Department of Archaeology at Southampton University.

He led the excavations here, at Fishbourne, from 1961-69, making sure the site and finds reports were written up within 2 years. The whole of the excavations and reports cost £12,140.

More can be read about his life in archaeology and publishing at the end of this display.

MARGARET RULE CBE

Margaret Rule was born 27 September 1928. She gained her degree at Cambridge University and was a qualified and experienced archaeologist when the Palace was discovered in 1960. She became the Palace's first Curator in 1965.

During the '60s she was a very active excavator, working with Alec Down in 1966, on land north of St Mary's Hospital, Chichester. Her discoveries seem to indicate an early Roman military presence. In 1967 she was involved in the excavations in Lyon Street. She was inspired by the inscriptions found in North Street in 1723, which recorded the dedication of a temple, to Neptune and Minerva, by a guild of workmen with the authority of Tiberius Claudius (To)gidubnus, King and Legate.

Margaret Rule was also involved with the work at Chichester Cathedral, in 1966-67, when it was decided to underpin the foundations of the buttress at the east end of the cathedral. The mosaic border found there was lifted, backed with fibre glass and displayed in the cathedral. It is possibly 2nd Century.

More can be discovered about her work and achievements at the end of this display.

BENEFACTORS AND DIRECTORS II

The three people primarily responsible for Fishbourne Roman Palace's excavation and preservation all received acclaim for their accomplishments in their lives and chosen careers.

IVAN D MARGARY FSA

Ivan Margary served in the First World War as a lieutenant in the Royal Sussex Regiment and was wounded in action at Gallipoli.

In 1927 he inherited a large property and a sum of money from his uncle, Sydney Larnick. Also in 1927, he joined the Sussex Archaeological Society and in 1932 became a Fellow of The Society of Antiquities in London.

Much of his inheritance was donated as gifts to the Archaeological Societies of Sussex, Surrey and Kent, and to the Society of Antiquities. He and his family were also generous benefactors to the village of Felbridge in Sussex.

He wrote two volumes of 'Roman Roads in Britain', published in 1955 and 1957. He also wrote about Roman history and was a keen and knowledgeable excavator. His researches included the area around the 'Long Man of Wilmington', which is carved into the northern side of Windover Hill. In 1928 he assisted in the excavation of a Roman bloomery at Whalesbeach and Stone Field Forestrow and helped to date that site to the second century.

PROFESSOR SIR BARRY CUNLIFFE CBE

Barry Cunliffe excavated in Britain, France and Spain. In Britain he excavated the Iron Age hill fort at Danebury, Hampshire from 1969-88. Other sites included Hengistbury Head ,Dorset; Mount Batten, Devon; Le Câtlin, Jersey; and Le Yaudet, Brittany. These excavations reflect his interest in the communities of Atlantic Europe during the Iron Age. This interest generated a number of publications on European trade at that time.

He was Professor of Archaeology at Oxford University from 1972 to 2007, and was knighted on 17 June 2006. He has also served as President of the Society of Antiquities and President of the Council of British Archaeology. He is currently a Commissioner of English Heritage and a Trustee Director of the Mary Rose Trust.

At the time of writing he is still active with excavations at Brading, Isle of Wight. His book, 'Europe between the Oceans 9000BC-AD1000' was published in 2008. Barry Cunliffe lives in Oxford with his wife and two cats.

MARGARET RULE CBE

After her work in Fishbourne and in Chichester, Margaret became involved in the raising of the Mary Rose, Henry VIII's flagship. It had sunk off Portsmouth in 1545 on its way to engage the French fleet, which had already landed on the Isle of Wight.

Alexander McKee, a student whom she met at one of her evening classes at Fishbourne, told her of his interest in looking for the Mary Rose. Intrigued, she joined his team. She trained the team of divers to record what they saw under water and she also learned to dive herself. In 1982, the skeletal remains of the Mary Rose were raised from 50 feet below sea-level. Over 10,000 well preserved items had been excavated, including weapons, clothes and a backgammon set.

She became Archaeological Director in charge of the operation for the Mary Rose Trust until 1994. She was honoured with a CBE in 1995 and the National Maritime Museum awarded her its Caird Medal. In 2001, a Portsmouth University accommodation block was named after her.

FRIENDS, ROMANS AND COUNTRYMEN

WHAT HAPPENED IN
1967

- "Torrey Canyon" hits rocks off Cornwall: ecological disaster

- First heart transplant by Dr Christian Barnard in South Africa

- Six day war in Middle East

- Stalin's daughter defects to the West

- Library opens in Chichester

The excavations and the ensuing publicity had a great impact on the village of Fishbourne and the surrounding area. Some people feared the worst...

RESIDENTS OPPOSE FISHBOURNE PALACE PROPOSALS

Not all the villagers felt like this however.

"...I think I first heard about it on the radio and it was very exciting to have such an important discovery made right on our doorsteps. We used to walk over from Deeside to see what was going on. There was a rush to see everything that we could. It was very open: we just walked in. There were a lot of people digging and scraping."

"...we in Fishbourne were using the excavations as the main entertainment for our summer visitors, and at weekends there was usually quite a crowd standing watching the diggers."

"Looking back, it is not only the excitement of the discoveries I remember but the friends I made and the comic incidents too – three elderly gentlemen leaping up and down on the pavement outside our garden for instance, in an attempt to see over our wall, and Mrs. Robertson-Ritchie's account of driving to the British Museum with four skeletons on the back seat of her car."

ARCHAEOLOGISTS WANT TO DIG LOCAL GARDENS

The gentlemen were trying to see into the gardens because the site of the Palace extended under the road and houses on the main street of the village. This led to pleas from the archaeologists for villagers to "lend their gardens".

Several trenches had been dug in our garden. The first trench, in summer 1962 produced the corner of a large bath with a denarius of Vespasian (AD73) lying on the floor.

The following winter he (Barry Cunliffe) and two or three others excavated part of a hypocaust when snow was on the ground, such was their enthusiasm, and my mother heated soup while they dripped on the kitchen floor!

Anne Blakeney

"...and I know they came at Christmas because one year they had dug our front garden and just left the path to the door standing up between the two excavations. We had a drinks party one morning and my husband was afraid someone might fall either on their way in or out. We had such a lot of fun with it."

WATER MAINS AND ROMANS

WHAT HAPPENED IN
1960

- First telephone conversation by satellite.

- First successful demonstration of the laser.

- Beatles first public performance at Kaiser Keller in Hamburg

- Rome Olympic Games.

- Princess Margaret marries Anthony Armstrong-Jones

- First Cosmonaut

- John F Kennedy elected President of United States

- First episode of Coronation Street

For many years, sherds of Roman pottery, fragments of roofing tiles and tessarae have been unearthed by ploughing the fields around the village of Fishbourne.

In 1805, when digging by the roadside (now the A259), a tessellated pavement was found. In the middle was part of the base of a column. These came to light during the construction of a house at the Bull's Head, Fishbourne . When the house was sold, it was marketed as being "delightfully situated....... and boasting a curious Roman pavement 13ft square".

Later, in 1812, "certain subterranean remains" were unearthed.

In 1835, the Reverend Horsfield wrote: "There can be no doubt that the Roman patricians and chiefs had villas in the neighbourhood, which time will someday bring to light".

Early in the 20th century, the Reverend N. Shaw started to collect and record the Roman remains of his parish.

More occupation rubbish was discovered in the silt filling the Roman harbour in the watercress beds and along the main road towards Chichester.

One hundred and twenty five years later, the Reverend Horsfield's prediction proved true.

Early in 1960,a skin-diver found Roman building rubbish in the Mill pond south of the village near the harbour.

Later that year, the Chichester City Water Department's labour gang was excavating a trench through fields north of Fishbourne.

The driver of the digger began to cut his way through what was obviously Roman material, and stopped to report his finds. Fortunately, after a previous encounter, the team knew what to do.

Mr. Alfred Burgess, Engineer and manager of Chichester Corporation Waterworks from 1945 to1963 recalls:

"I was amazed one wet Sunday (in 1959) to find a lady and a gentleman down in the muddy trench, pinning labels to the walls where they had found items of interest, while a baby in the pushchair above remained calmly reconciled, as though it was an everyday occurrence.

After a while, the parents broke off from their preoccupation to give me one of their visiting cards and it remained in my desk until the initial findings at Fishbourne."

Extract from "Portsmouth Water 1857-2007, 150 years of service" by Andy Neve and Mike Hedges.
Reproduced by kind permission of Portsmouth Water Company.

Mr. Burgess phoned Mr and Mrs Rule, the couple from the muddy trench the previous year.

Arthur Rule later described the ensuing events:

"My wife and myself were to be the fortunate people who discovered the interesting and extremely important archaeological remains of Roman Fishbourne.

In May 1960, we received a telephone call from the Chief Engineer of the Chichester Water Board advising us that they were excavating a trench to carry an 18" water main from the pumping station at Fishbourne to Wittering.

On inspecting the section revealed by the trench, we were amazed to see a mass of Roman roofing tiles, the foundations of three walls, a mosaic pavement, a tessellated corridor and many other signs of a large masonry building.

It was extremely fortunate that the trench had exposed one of the most interesting Roman discoveries found in Britain for a long while".

"the 18" water main, Fishbourne. Picture taken a day or two before exposing broken tiles. May 1969. Picture courtesy of Portsmouth water.

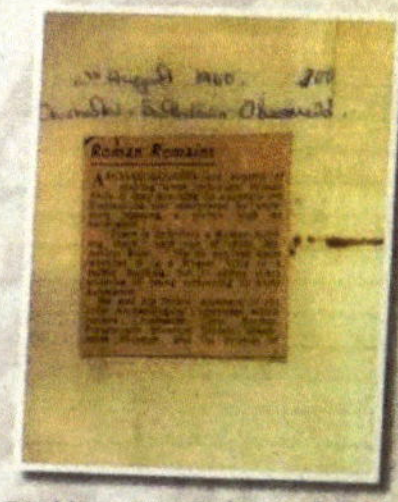

"At the time of the discovery of Fishbourne Palace I was Treasurer of what was called 'The Joint Archaeological Committee' of which Margaret Rule and her husband Arthur were driving forces.

While not claiming to have turned the first sod on the site, mine may actually have been among the first half dozen, I was a member of the original party which the Rules assembled on the weekend after the first report of finds of tiles was sent in by workmen from the Water Company.

I worked there on a number of weekends after the original ground-breaking; I can recall on at least one occasion driving Barry Cunliffe to the Chichester station so he could catch a train back to University on Sunday evening, in my Austin7! What a claim to fame by proxy!

It was indeed an exciting time!"

Extract form Mr W S Bainbridge's memories of the original Fishbourne digs.

A report was made to the Civic Society and with the permission of the site owner Mr F Ledger, rescue excavations were planned for Easter 1961 under the direction of Barry Cunliffe, a local Cambridge Undergraduate .

The appeal for "diggers" began.

TRENCHES AND TROWELS I

WHAT HAPPENED IN
1963

- John F Kennedy assassinated

- Martin Luther King civil rights march in Washington

- "I have a dream speech"

- Inauguration of Picasso Museum in Barcelona

- Profumo scandal

- Great train robbery: £2,631784 stolen

- "Beatles" first No 1: "Please Please me"

- Chichester Museum opens in old corn store

The Working Day:

At the start of the week, Barry Cunliffe would talk all the volunteers through the plans for the week ahead.

The duties of the diggers varied.

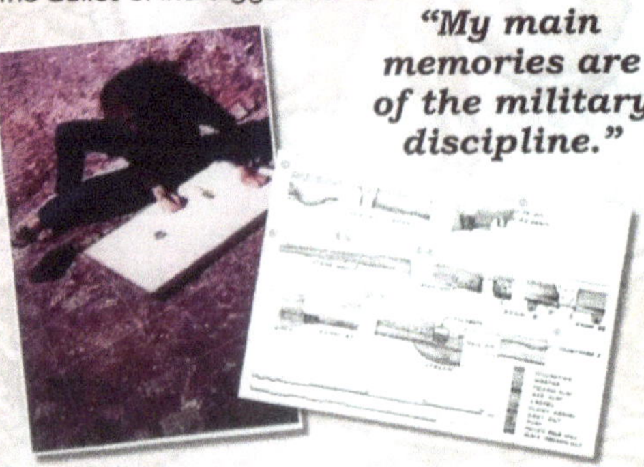

Archaeology is destructive by it's very nature so plans (horizontal recording) and section drawings (vertical recording) must be kept of the site.

"My main memories are of the military discipline."

Margaret Rule cleaning the Boy and Dolphin mosaic for photography.

"My only memories are of the Beatles music and lots of mud!"

The diggers' day involved excavating in many different situations...

Being a digger was not all digging!

Breaktime!

"The Brummies I worked with were adept at timing things to get the pints first onto the bar at lunchtime."

TRENCHES AND TROWELS II

Health and safety was an issue back in the 60s too..

"Working with hand tools in farm rich loam is not without its hazards, and volunteers are advised to consult their family doctor about the advisability of having anti-tetanus inoculations before taking part in any excavations".

"Volunteers should have soft rubber-soled shoes, and each person should have their own pointing trowel with a 4 to 5-inch blade. All other tools and equipment are available on the site."

Not all safety precautions were followed however. Diggers were often barefoot.

"I went as part of a group from my school as a way of finishing the term by way of doing something interesting. We stayed in a school and spent the days working on the site. It must have been 1964. I remember it was hard work as I had to fill a wheelbarrow with earth and wheel it to a tip and then repeat the exercise for much of the time"

Despite the dangers, most diggers seem to have happy memories of their time at Fishbourne:

"A lovely day at Fishbourne.... got irritated with a young American girl whose interest in archaeology was infinitesimal but whose interest in boys was excessive."

"I can supply you with memories – of the dreadful jam sandwiches that we made before starting out – of the shock of realising that, having dug for the penultimate week, we had to spend the final week filling in all the trenches."

"Fishbourne in those days was a fairly relaxed affair. . . it seemed to be run as a community project – people of all sorts, which made for an interesting atmosphere but needed more supervisors. . . but it was good fun, and Barry took good care to make sure that everyone got a site tour weekly to know what was going on."

DIGGERS AND DITCHES

WHAT HAPPENED IN
1961

- Yuri Gagarin first man in space

- Building of Berlin Wall starts

- Attempt by US to overthrow Fidel Castro at Bay of Pigs

- "Asterix and Obelix" first comic strip in weekly magazine called "Pilote"

- New railway station opens in Chichester

It was apparent from the early finds that the site was an important one, and that a large number of volunteer diggers would be required. Notices were placed in archaeological journals, and word soon spread.

Barry Cunliffe was appointed to lead the excavations and he brought with him a small team of experienced archaeologists, who would act as site supervisors, training the volunteers in the many and varied tasks that needed to be performed.

Application forms arrived from all over the world, as a week or two (or an entire season!) at Fishbourne was considered to be an exciting and interesting way to spend the summer.

I can hardly imagine a better way for a teenager from about 16 and upwards to spend part of a summer or Easter holiday than helping on a "dig"….

In the end we found what we wanted; a dig for which untrained volunteers were needed, accommodation and food were being provided for a very reasonable sum, and the dates were right – schoolchildren can of course only go in the holidays…..

The dig was on the site of a Roman villa at Fishbourne, near Chichester, and accommodation (and a daily cook), were being provided in the secondary modern school in Chichester. The diggers had to bring camp beds and bedding, their own china and cutlery, and a 5in. pointed trowel. Clothing taken should of course be kept to a minimum.

Extracts from an article in The Daily Telegraph, 1961

"Some of us who could not dig took stools and buckets and old toothbrushes and sat in the field washing the fragments of pottery the diggers brought us in their boxes. It was all very informal and we were on the spot to see anything of interest that turned up."

Rita Blakeney

Amateurs share in the excitement. They are also attracted by working in the open air and concentrating on a job that is quite different from their normal occupations. There are other attractions. At Fishbourne, for example there is the Chichester Festival [Theatre], which helps to explain why the dig is popular with foreign volunteers from France, Germany, Yugoslavia and even the United States.

The Observer Magazine, July 4th 1965

CABBAGES AND FISHCAKES

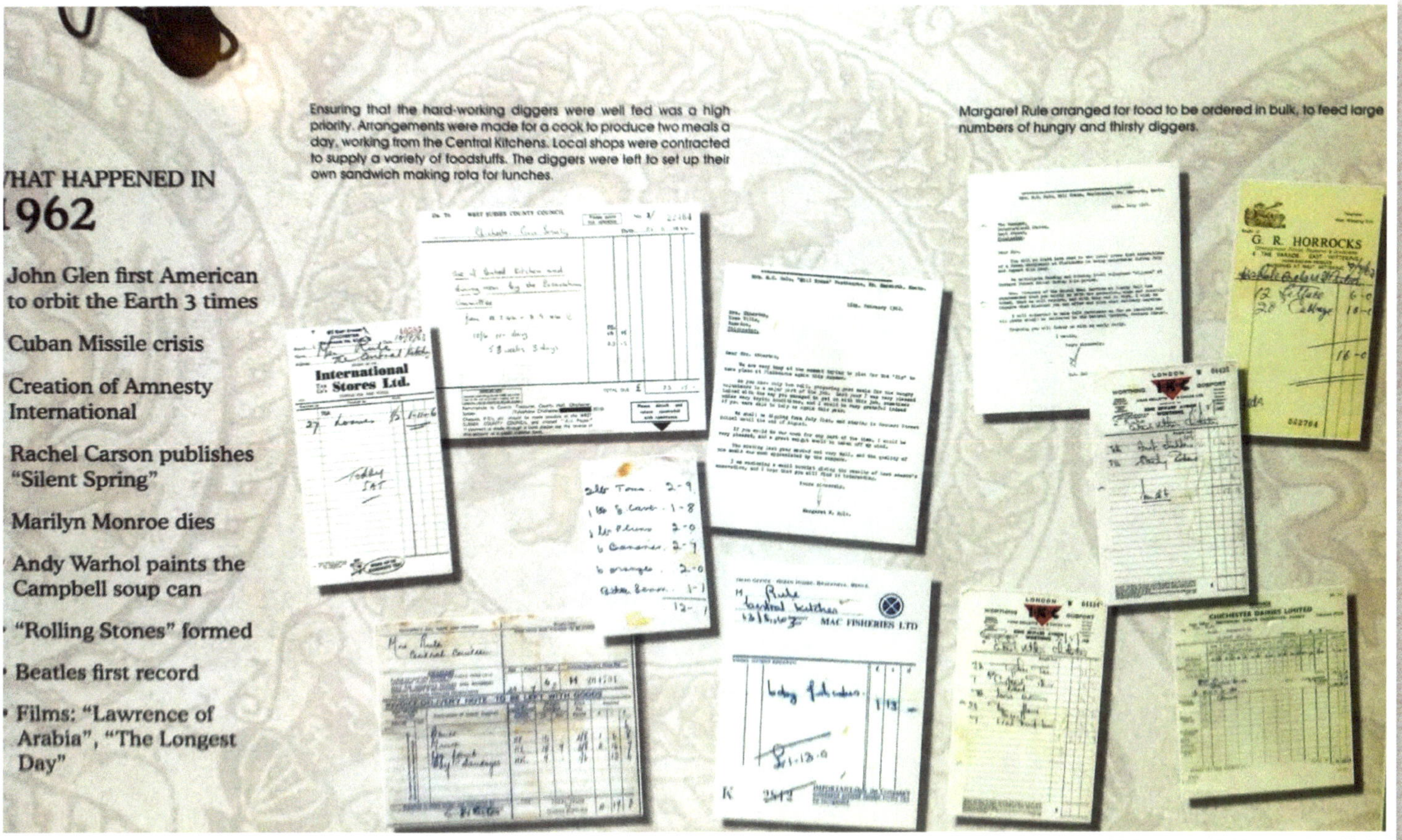

Ensuring that the hard-working diggers were well fed was a high priority. Arrangements were made for a cook to produce two meals a day, working from the Central Kitchens. Local shops were contracted to supply a variety of foodstuffs. The diggers were left to set up their own sandwich making rota for lunches.

Margaret Rule arranged for food to be ordered in bulk, to feed large numbers of hungry and thirsty diggers.

WHAT HAPPENED IN 1962

John Glen first American to orbit the Earth 3 times

Cuban Missile crisis

Creation of Amnesty International

Rachel Carson publishes "Silent Spring"

Marilyn Monroe dies

Andy Warhol paints the Campbell soup can

"Rolling Stones" formed

Beatles first record

Films: "Lawrence of Arabia", "The Longest Day"

ROMANCE AMID THE RUINS

With many of the young men and women working alongside each other for many seasons, it is not surprising that many romances blossomed, some leading to marriage.

As Barry Cunliffe wrote in the introduction to the Excavation Report,

"The frequency with which the young ladies married the men shows, perhaps, that the hard work did not entirely overshadow the social life."

We believe that nine couples met and married as a result of working at Fishbourne, and two of these have agreed to share their stories.

John Peter Wild met his future wife, Felicity at the very start of the excavations.

"I joined Barry's small team at Easter 1961, the initial excavation, and supervised in summer 1961, Felicity's first digging season at Fishbourne. She returned to supervise in 1962, when I took over from Gavin Brown as assistant director. We returned to dig, for the last time, in 1963."

David Baker, the site photographer, did not actually meet his future wife at Fishbourne, but their romance developed whilst working on the site:

"We actually met, famously, in a Napoleonic cess-pit in the angle of the Landgate and the main wall at Portchester Castle during Barry Cunliffe's July 1961 excavations - not at Fishbourne where I worked on the April 1961 trial trenches in complete ignorance of her existence. As you know, I was photographer for the main Fishbourne work and much of that at Portchester.

Evelyn (ex-Portsmouth College of Art) drew several of the mosaics during the excavations as well as that large acrylic one of the Dolphin pavement that (I believe) now hangs in the exhibition area. She also acted as photographer's assistant and the rest is history."

Another couple whose love grew whilst digging at Fishbourne were Beric Morley and Judith Hatfield (known to all as Hattie). Phillip Burstow refers to this in his diary:

"I spent all afternoon with Hattie. She had been on site several seasons and is a psychologist by profession. She is engaged to Beric, now supervising the interesting cutting in the courtyard."

It seems that love was definitely in the air at Fishbourne, and the tradition continues – Richard Jones and Naomi Sykes met during excavations that took place in the 1990s, and are still together now.

David Baker on the photo tower!

CAMPS AND SCHOOL

The diggers came from all corners of the world so had to be housed. Orchard Street School in Chichester came to the rescue and allowed an indoor camp to be set up in the school buildings. Bed and breakfast accommodation was available for those who required a more comfortable situation!

"I have memories of sleeping at a school (was it Central School?). On another occasion we camped out in the Shippams garden in Boxgrove and hitch-hiked to Fishbourne each day."

"sleeping on a a lilo that deflated by about 3 am each morning" LM

"In her organizing capacity, Mrs Rule had to find 60 persons to work on the site for six weeks. They had to be fed and found accommodation and she also had to arrange for their welfare. Then there were arrangements to be made where the tools, equipment and 101 other things needed during the digging season were concerned."

"Free indoor camping accommodation is available from July 23rd to August 31st in Orchard Street School, Chichester, approximately 1 mile from the site. A camping site for tents is available in a field adjacent to the school. The school buildings contain adequate facilities with hot and cold water, toilets etc. Volunteers will need their own sleeping equipment (camp bed and/or sleeping bag.) There are many restaurants in Chichester where meals at various prices can be obtained.

A list of Bed and Breakfast accommodation in Chichester can be supplied on request.

From July 29th-August 31st full board can be provided at Orchard Street School for £3-0-0 per week inclusive. This includes Hot Breakfast, packed lunch and hot dinner at night. Those people who wish to have these meals should book them in advance on the enrolment form, and they will be expected to join in a "sandwich making" and washing up rota".

The 60-80 volunteers a day who took part (once peaking at 120) lived in moderate squalor in the classrooms of a primary school in Chichester and were expected to walk the two kilometres to and from the site every day. This they did with good grace arriving on site (it was the height of the 1960's flower-power revolution), their hair-bands suitably decorated, leaving the front gardens en route increasingly depleted as the season wore on.

Barry Cunliffe, Introduction, Facing the Palace

BEACHES AND BEER

WHAT HAPPENED IN
1964

- Aswan high dam under construction in Egypt: UNESCO decides to save Abu Simbel Temple

- Anglo-French agreement reached for construction of "Chunnel"

- Harold Wilson Prime Minister

- Nobel Peace prize to Martin Luther King

- Civil Rights Bill approved in US

- Nelson Mandela sentenced to life imprisonment

- "Beatles" arrive in US.

- Premiere of "A Hard Day's Night"

- "Mods and Rockers"

The social life of the diggers centred, then as now, around the various pubs in Fishbourne. They did, however, venture further afield to the beach and to Chichester and the theatre. On a more academic note, lectures were provided in the evening and visits to other Roman sites were organized.

The accommodation at the school was fairly basic, although attempts were made to try to make it more homely

During the long hot summers, the diggers often went to the nearby beaches to cool of at the end of the day.

They also found other ways to occupy their time, visiting Chichester, parties, or just relaxing.

ACTORS AND ARCHAEOLOGISTS

WHAT HAPPENED IN
1965

- Winston Churchill dies aged 90
- Ban on TV cigarette advertising
- Alexei Leonov first man to walk in space
- R C Duncan patents the world's first disposable nappy
- BP strikes oil in North sea. Petrol 5 shilling per gallon (25p)
- Post Office tower opens in London
- First "Kentucky Fried Chicken" opens in UK
- Great New York Blackout
- Ronnie Biggs escapes from Wandsworth Prison to Brazil
- "Beatles" awarded MBE
- Chichester: Bishop Luffa school and College of Further Education opens; new bus station

The Excavation coincided with the opening of The Chichester Festival Theatre and since archaeology was then considered to be a somewhat refined cultural phenomenon occasions were engineered for the two groups of performers to meet. A trip to the excavations became an afternoon out for off duty actors while tired diggers paid a return visit to watch the actors at work in the evening.

From Facing the Palace, foreword by Barry Cunliffe

Some of the actors made quite dramatic appearances. Barry Cunliffe describes one such moment in *Facing the Palace*.

One memorable occasion was the arrival on site of Dame Sybil Thorndike. To get to the gate it was necessary to cross a stream on a bridge made of two railway sleepers – a difficult task for an elderly lady. Once across she paused to get her breath, making dramatic use of the occasion to act out a sweeping survey of the scene and then, when the moment was right, booming "Is this the Roman Excavations?" ensuring that all eyes were on her as she made her entry. Others came too. Sir Michael Redgrave, after what we assumed to have been a challenging lunch, was just saved from stepping off the edge of a deep trench.

Laurence Olivier was seen to offer cigarettes to the diggers with an unassuming "They're named after me you know".

"Actor Laurence Olivier (1907-89) had a cigarette brand named after him. The deal for the Olivier-tipped cigarettes made by Gallaher, was that he received two pence for every 1,000 cigarettes sold. He was a £2,000 advance against the first years royalties – money for old smoke.

He also received 500 packs of 20 every week for his own use and to distribute to his friends – a handsome 10,000 cigarettes a week. Olivier was loyal to his brand."

Taken from "The Cigarette Book" by Chris Harrold and Fletcher Watkins.

Many of the diggers have happy recollections of the theatre:

Wed Aug 28th 1963.

I went at 7.0 to the Festival Theatre and for 5/- got standing room and saw "St. Joan" with Joan Plowright as St Joan.

Philip Burstow

We slept on the floor of a school in Spring (??) Street when we were not sleeping outside the theatre to queue for theatre tickets.

D.C.

I saw The Royal Hunt of the Sun at Chichester Theatre, and Laurence Olivier in Othello, the tickets for which I slept out on the pavement.

BR

I remember the late Dame Sybil Thorndike, Sir Lewis Casson, Derek Nimmo etc from Chichester Theatre peering at us in the trenches!

RB

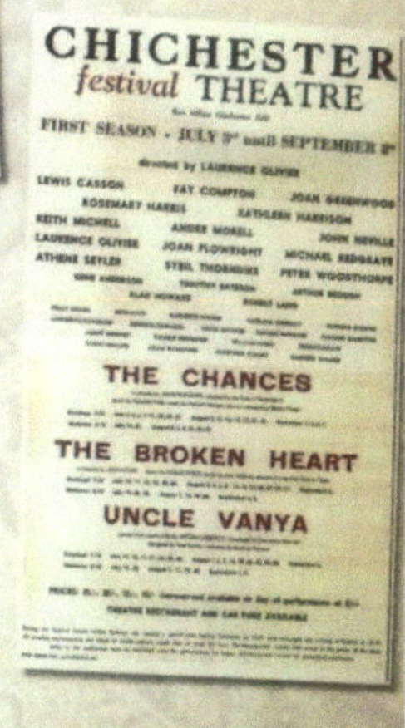

BONES AND BURIALS

Several skeletons were found during the excavations, none of them Roman. However, they aroused a great deal of interest, both among the museum fraternity and the local police. If any human remains are found by archaeologists, the local coroner has to be informed, and the authorities must be satisfied that no crime has been committed.

One skeleton was unearthed in 1963, the year of the Great Train Robbery. The police were more interested than usual, as they had the task of checking any disturbed ground to make sure the money had not been buried there.

In 1964 the discovery of another skeleton caused excitement for another reason. Mr. Looker, one of the diggers tells the story:

Summer 1964

In a grave cut into the opus signinum floor of the North Wing, lay a skeleton being excavated, not quite ready to be lifted.

Senior police officers arrived at the dig, concerned for the skeletons safety: Chichester had a practicing coven of witches and there had been instances of graveyards being desecrated. The date was the eve of the first of May – WALPURGIS NIGHT– a high point in the witchcraft calendar, the officers feared that the coven would like to get their hands on "pagan" bones for use in their revels that night.

Two volunteers spent the night sleeping either side of the remains (dubbed YORICK; not very original) and the bones were decorated with joss sticks which gave an eerie glow to the proceedings.

I took the sinister side, alas I no longer remember the name of the fellow digger who took the dexter.

NOTHING HAPPENED, no awful hags arrived to carry off the bones, I don't think I was disappointed!!!

Michael G Looker

"A Roman skeleton has been found at the Fishbourne Roman villa site by William H. Hogan (schoolteacher from Washington D.C. U.S.A.) who with his friend (on right) George Constantinople (a former student of Mr. Hogan), are lending a hand with other students to uncover more of this vast Roman villa site."

FILM CREWS AND FOOTAGE

WHAT HAPPENED IN
1966

- Mao Zedong cultural revolution in China

- Indira Ghandi prime minister of India

- Mary Quant: the mini skirt

- Hippies

- England World Cup Champions

- "Star Trek"

The discovery and excavation of the Palace at Fishbourne aroused a great deal of media interest, with articles appearing in the local, national and international press. Television crews were also frequent visitors to the site throughout the 1960s.

In 1963 a BBC film unit arrived to record a programme called "The Romans Came to Fishbourne", to be presented by Professor Ian Richmond and Barry Cunliffe.

Phillip Burstow, a regular digger, recorded the event in his diary.

Wed August 14th 1963.

..Today Professor Richmond came and I think the B.B.C. did a film of us in case of rain tomorrow. There are B.B.C. vans en masse in our field.

Thurs Aug 15th 1963.

..At 5.0 most were sent home. About then the B.B.C. did a recording of the programme.

The programme was to be live but the recording was so good that it was finally used. Barry Cunliffe and Professor Richmond did the talking and very well as far as I could hear from my position.

The Central Office of Information came to film a programme about the excavations for their "This Week in Britain" series, which was broadcast on the World Service.

Rita Blakeney, a local resident who had allowed Barry Cunliffe to excavate in her garden, took part in the filming. Here she explains how it was done.

We agreed to be filmed having a tea out-of-doors. When the day came it rained heavily, but the next day the "tea-party" took place at short notice at 9.00am. The film was produced in five editions, each one introduced by a reporter from the country in which it was to be shown, so I poured out my cold tea for each of the five girls in turn, and between takes returned the stone-cold tea to the teapot.

As Richard Bradley, waist-deep in the trench, had already cleaned the tiled bath floor on which he stood, for the photography he had to fling up shovelfuls of earth from a carefully hidden bucket, to give an appearance of excavation in progress

A break from filming, drinking hot tea from flasks

Filming in Rita's garden: Richard Bradley in the trench, and camera on the lawn

Other companies, including the Rank Organisation also came to film at Fishbourne.

FISHBOURNE TO FAME

THE SITE SUPERVISORS OF THE 1960s

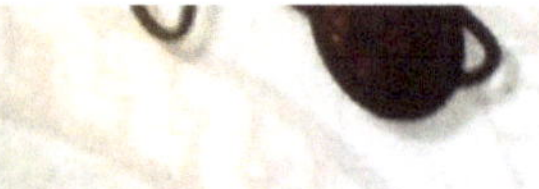

RICHARD BRADLEY	A.J.PARKER
KEVIN GREENE	NIGEL SUNTER

MARTIN HENIG	MALCOLM TODD
IAN McLELLAN	JOHN PETER WILD
BERIC MORLEY	PETER WEBSTER
REV TONY NORTON	MARTIN BIDDLE

WHAT THEY DID NEXT!

Professor Richard Bradley – Barry Cunliffe's right hand man on the Fishbourne dig. He went on to be Professor of Pre-Historic Archaeology at Reading University and wrote a number of books, including "An Archaeology of Natural Places".

Dr Kevin Greene is a leading lecturer at Newcastle University. He has written many books. One of his best known is "An Introduction to Archaeology" which is used by most first year archaeology students.

Dr Martin Henig is now Professor at the Institute of Archaeology at Oxford University. He has also written many books, including "Art in Roman Britain" and "Religion in Roman Britain".

Dr Ian McLellan went on to be a medical doctor and has visited Fishbourne with The Gillingham Archaeology Society.

Beric Morley went into teaching and quickly moved into the world of archaeology. On the 60s dig at Fishbourne he met his future wife, Judith. He has become a regular fixture alongside Tony Robinson on Channel 4s Time Team, as their historic buildings expert. Sadly, he now suffers from Alzheimer's disease.

Rev. Tony Norton was a site supervisor and assistant director at Fishbourne for many years, whilst studying for to become a minister. One of his first duties after his ordination was to perform the marriage of Beric and Judith Morley. Tony married a fellow site supervisor, Caroline Picard.

Dr A.J.Parker is a lecturer at the Department of Archaeology and Anthropology at Bristol University. He has written many books including "Ancient Shipwrecks of the Mediterranean and the Roman Provinces".

Nigel Sunter became an architect, specialising in conservation and the alteration of historic buildings. He has helped to secure the future of many historic buildings.

Professor Malcolm Todd was a lecturer in Archaeology at Exeter University and then went on to be Principal of Trevelyan College, Durham. His fields of interest are the Roman Provinces, late antiquity and the migration period in Europe. He has also written many articles and books including "Roman Britain 55BC – AD400".

Dr John Peter Wild is an Honorary Research Fellow of Archaeology at Manchester University. His interest is archaeological textiles, and has written books including "The Textile Industries of Roman Britain". He met his wife, Felicity during the 1960s excavations.

Professor Martin Biddle is a Fellow of Hertford College, Oxford and lectures in Medieval Archaeology at Oxford University. He has also written many books.

Dr Peter Webster is a lecturer at Cardiff University. His field is archaeology and the ancient world, specialising in Roman Samian pottery and ceramics. He has also written books including "Roman Samian Pottery in Britain" He also met his wife, Miss Joanne Waring at the Fishbourne dig.

OPENINGS AND OFFICIALS

WHAT HAPPENED IN
1968

- Students riots in Paris

- "Prague Spring" uprising

- Martin Luther King assassinated in Memphis

- Robert Kennedy assassinated

- Jackie Kennedy marries Onassis

- First quartz watch

- Films: "2001 A Space Odyssey", "Rosemary's baby"

The North Wing Cover Building

Thanks to a generous donation by Ivan Margary, a building was erected to protect and display the mosaic floors of the north wing of the Palace.

The Museum was financed by the Sunday Times, which had regularly run features on the excavations during the 1960s.

The Opening

Fishbourne Roman Palace was officially opened at 3.00pm on Thursday 30th May 1968, by Ivan Margary.

Barry Cunliffe (who had been appointed Professor of Archaeology at Southampton University in 1966) then spoke, thanking the team of volunteers that had made the excavations possible.

Philip Burstow described the day in his diary:

"At 3.0 the opening ceremony began presided over by the Bishop of Chichester. He began the proceedings and then called on Margary to speak from a small raised dais. Margary in a very homely relaxed civilised way spoke of the great work and praised the various bodies who had carried it out. He himself has given well over £100,000 towards it and he was in a great state of delight today when I spoke to him afterwards."

"Then Barry Cunliffe spoke. The beard was there but sober dark clothing as befits a professor. He spoke well indeed humorously and gratefully to the 700 or so diggers of which I am delighted to have been one."

"At the opening of the Palace to the public in 1968 my mother and I were stewards: I shall never forget that first weekend, the Whitsun bank holiday. with a TV programme and a Sunday Times colour supplement producing thousands of visitors: there were traffic jams on the main road (and road widening took place faster than one would have believed possible) and at the railway crossing, and I remember standing at the entrance to the museum explaining its layout to the waiting queues, over and over until I wondered if I was making any sense"

Rita Blakeney

PRINCES AND POLITICIANS

Visitors came from far and wide when the Palace opened in 1968

Between June and November 1968, Fishbourne had been visited by a quarter of a million people. Caernarvon Castle received the same number of visitors, but over an entire year!

Fishbourne was visited by members of the Royal Families of Europe

Prince Charles came for a private visit with King Constantine and Queen Anne – Marie of Greece and his favourite uncle Lord Mountbatten, just before Christmas, a few months before he became Prince of Wales.

His father, The Duke of Edinburgh was also visited some time later.

Also, King Gustav of Sweden, an eminent amateur archaeologist, accompanied by his grand-daughter Margareta came for a 90 minute tour of the site, guided by the curator, Margaret Rule. He was believed to have said "Fishbourne ranks as one of Britain's most important Roman sites."

The World of Politics

Jennie Lee was a very active Member of Parliament and Minister for the Arts. She was instrumental in the formation of the Open University, and later became Baroness Lee of Asheridge.

She expressed an interest in a visit to Fishbourne and a private tour was arranged for her.

The World of Cinema and Television

Many of the stars of the time visited the site with interest.

CHARLTON HESTON

SPIKE MILLIGAN

DIANA DORS

DEREK NIMMO

HUGHIE GREEN

WILLIAM ROCHE

MARGOT BRYANT

BETH ALBERGE

The World of Pop Music

The world famous Rolling Stones, Mick Jagger and Keith Richards visited, accompanied by Marianne Faithfull.

The archives give an insight to how huge and demanding the management role undertaken by Mrs Rule was. She organised the day to day food supplies, the accommodation for the diggers and the number of diggers required each day. She handled the correspondence, including dealing with The Association for Cultural Exchange, who had eight students coming over from America wanting to dig at Fishbourne. The day to day journal written by G P Burstow reveals that diggers came from across the globe, even as far away as Australia. Mrs Rule became the first Director of Fishbourne Roman Palace and her responsibilities were vast and varied, including giving a guided tour of the site to King Gustav of Sweden.

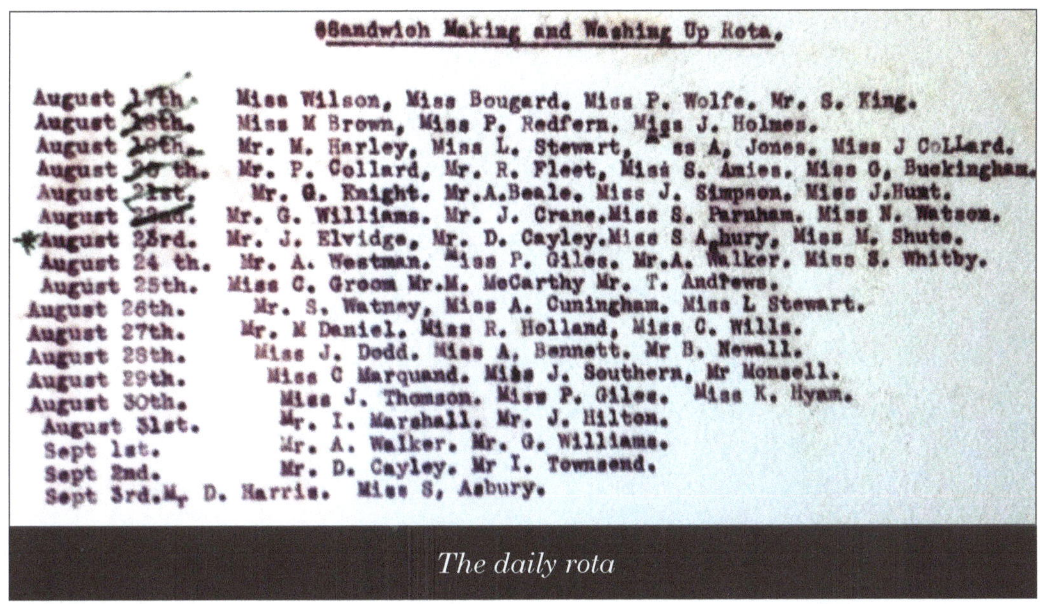

The daily rota

What the diggers did in their spare time can be viewed on the boards entitled 'Actors and Archaeologists' and' Beaches and Beer'. Relationships blossomed and nine couples met and eventually married (Romance amid the Ruins).

Several diggers went on to academic success.

Martin Henig became a Professor of the Institute of Archaeology at Oxford University. He has been a busy author writing many books, including Art in Roman Britain and Religion in Roman Britain.

Beric Morley was seen regularly on the Channel Four TimeTeam programme. The excavations coincided with the opening of the Chichester Festival Theatre (Actors and Archaeologists). This led to a good trip out for the off duty actors, including *Laurence Olivier* and *Joan Plowright*, and the diggers were able to take a trip out to the theatre in the evenings. The diggers were even invited to a cheese and wine party one Friday evening by the Mayor of Chichester.

Prince Charles and the *Duke of Edinburgh*, accompanied by the Prince's uncle, *Lord Mountbatten* (Princes and Politicians) were just a few of a number of dignitaries who visited the remains.

For many weeks after the opening of the Palace remains, the roads in to Fishbourne were regularly congested, and visitors queued patiently to view this wonderful and exciting discovery.

In conclusion, please view the two boards 'Benefactors and Directors' – for without the financial generosity of Ivan Margary, the Palace at Fishbourne in all probability would be resting under a housing estate, and dwell for a moment or two on what would be lost, not just to the visiting adult public, but also to the thousands of visiting schoolchildren who experience contact with the Romans through the education workshops and artefact handling of things made and used by people living nearly 2,000 years ago.

Footnote - The Sunday Times, through their then Managing Director, Dennis Hamilton, donated £15,000 for the laying out of the Fishbourne Palace Museum.

Chapter II

Fishbourne Roman Palace can still speak to us about a vanished age, but in hushed tones only. These tantalising murmurings lurk in numerous places in its museum where painted wall-plaster, samian pottery and a reconstructed palace room help to smother us with its opulence. This is compounded by the floors of mosaics within its North Wing. More silent voices dwell within the excavation reports of the 1960s and within the writings of historians of antiquity. More modern authors of history also have a voice of opinion. It is from within all of these sources, of past and present, which I will delve into to seek out possible answers to the most popular questions that have been asked of me during my time of engagement with visitors to the palace. The questions are numerous and many and include – Who lived at the palace? Why was it built at this location? When was it constructed? And why was it apparently abandoned? To be able to come to any conclusion to these questions, we have to take a backward glance through a window of history and view the developing change of culture and politics, born on the wind through the assent of Rome.

Roman Room

Painted wall-plaster

This is a modern reconstruction showing what one of the domestic rooms in the Palace may have looked like around AD 100. Although nothing is genuinely Roman, everything here is based on archaeological evidence from Fishbourne or elsewhere in the Western Roman Empire.

The painted wall plaster and mosaic floor are based on fragments found in rooms in the north wing of the Roman Palace.

Roman furniture was usually made from organic materials, so it rarely survives: carvings and wall paintings provide some of the best information about it.

Both the couch and wooden cabinet are copied from stone carvings. The former is from tombstones found in York and Chester. The source for the latter is a coffin found at Simpelveld in the Netherlands. The rectangular table is based on ones illustrated in wall painting from Pompeii and the circular table is similar to one found at Herculaneum.

Roman Room

Painted wall-plaster

Samian pottery

THE PEOPLE

The populace of Britannia were in close contact with continental Europe for many hundreds of years by using the avenues of trade and trade routes. Britannia had much to export: grain, cattle, hunting dogs, hides, slaves and minerals – including gold, silver and iron. In all probability it was a relatively peaceful island with the peace of the land occasionally disturbed by conflict between certain tribes, as their population grew, and as a consequence, good farming land became a premium.

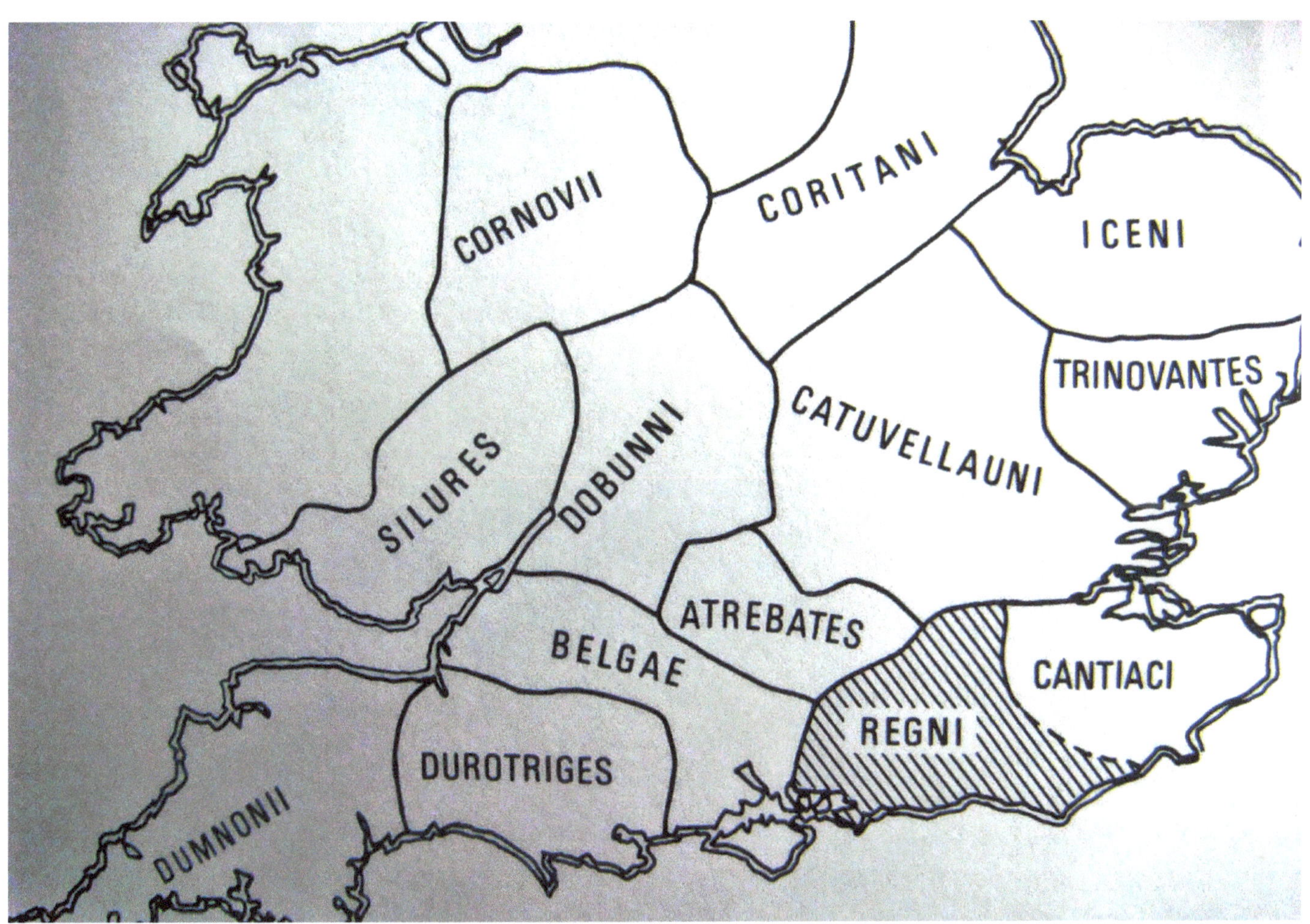

The tribes of central and southern England (B Cunliffe-the Regni)

The Roman world was also expanding, as was their consumer society and the need for raw materials and man-power increased. These economic reasons were interlocked with a complex political situation, all of which seemed to fall upon the shoulders of Julius Caesar. In 58 BC, Julius Caesar felt the need to bring the vast expanse of Gaul (France) as far north as the River Rhine under Roman control. Later, Caesar, believing that the Gauls were receiving military assistance from Britain, made arrangements for an assault, consisting of two Legions with supporting cavalry, in 55 BC on Britain. Caesar tells us in his 'Commentarii de Bello Gallico' (commentaries on the Gallic war) that the cavalry failed to cross the Channel due to an adverse tide and weather conditions. It was during Caesar's two assaults on Britain (55-54 BC) that the first signs of the footprints of Roman foreign policy in Britain were detected. In all probability Caesar made a determined effort in the south east of England (and later to the north east) to establish dynasties that would be loyal to Rome. Caesar would have offered gifts and gold subsidies to potential allies in exchange for 'hostages'. These hostages would have been young men from the ruling royal elite, escorted to Rome and educated in all things Roman. This would have been a learning curve of Roman culture, including Roman foreign policy and how to organise Roman administration. No doubt these young men would have become fluent in Latin. By the time of the arrival of the Roman Emperor Claudius' legions, in 43 AD, the education of 'hostages' had been ongoing for nearly 100 years. Prior to the Claudian invasion, it seems that political unrest and civil discord had focused one of the tribal elite of the Atrebates, by the name of Verica (Berikos), to flee to Rome for assistance. This situation, then, plus Claudius's political aspirations and the need to harness Britain's natural resources, of grain and minerals for the ever expanding Roman Empire, were the three main reasons for the appearance of the Roman Legions under the command of Aulus Plautius upon the shores of Britain. I can only imagine that the shivering of the soldiers was impacted with apprehension and fear, as they waded ashore through icy cold water, passing from the then known world into one that was only known through rumours, hearsay and supposition.

The classical historians of this period of the distant past seem only to offer us thoughts and explanations which are shrouded in a veil of ambiguity. Perhaps it is worth a paragraph or two reviewing the political atmosphere and aspirations of the neighbouring tribes which encased the territory of Verica's Atrebates tribe about the year 40 AD. It seems that there was a period of insecurity as dynasties changed following the death of powerful rulers. The tribal lands of Verica came under threat from military expeditions from the sons of Cunobelin (King of the Catuvellauni), Caratacus and Togidubnus. Cunobelin was in poor health around 40 AD and, perhaps, had died by 42 AD. History tells us that the Catuvellauni had been hostile towards the Trinovantes tribe and Cunobelin possibly ruled the joint Catuvellaunian/Trinovantian kingdom from Camulodunam (Colchester). The Catuvellauni were the most prominent tribe in the south of Britain and were leaders of the opposition against the Roman invasion. Therefore, this tribe had to be defeated and subdued before the region could be secured. Consequently Camulodunam was taken and subjugated under the command of the Roman Governor, Aulus Plautius. It seems that the Catuvellauni, at this period of time, were also in control of the Cantii/Cantiaci tribe whose territory occupied the south east corner of Britain which included Kent, Eastern Surrey, East Sussex and London, south of the Thames. They were bordered across the Thames by the Catuvellauni/Trinovantes tribes. The Cantii were defeated at the battle of the Medway, when the Romans used their Batavi mounted troops to cross the River Medway, and surprised the Britons. These mounted troops were again used when the Romans were confronted by the River Thames. It could well be that Adminius, a son of Canobelin, was forced to flee the country due to his pro-Roman tendencies (when administering the Cantii tribe on his father's behalf) but was installed as governor as repayment for his loyalty to Rome after the Cantii were subdued. As for the Trinovantes tribe, they seem to have lost their independence to the Catuvellauni around 9 AD; their territory was north of the Thames Estuary (the area around pre-Roman London) to the east coast of England and northwards into lower Suffolk. To their west were the lands of the Catuvellauni. In north western Suffolk and eastern Cambridgeshire were the lands of the Iceni tribe. They seemed to welcome the Romans, probably due to the destruction of their over-powerful neighbours, the Catuvellauni, although it seems that some factions within the Iceni were disillusioned with Rome's confirmation of Anterdios as the sole ruler of the Iceni. It could well be that the Catuvellauni were trying to move the south of Britain towards the development of a single kingdom. In all probability, the Catuvellauni were causing disruption within the Dobunni tribe. The Dobunni lands lay to the west of the aggressive Catuvellaunis and it seems that by 43 AD the tribe had divided into two. In the north east, from the southern side of the Stroud valley to north eastern Gloucestershire, Romanised coinage were recognised, but in Avon and southern Gloucestershire the coins were of a native type. With the defeat of the Catuvellauni by the marauding Roman legions, it seems that the Dubonni surrendered themselves and consequently became a Roman 'client' tribe.

If we delve into the past of the Atrebates, Belgae and Regni tribes, a more settled and perhaps an interlocking relationship can be possibly recognised as a large, integrated society, bounded together by beneficial trading with Europe and the Mediterranean through civilised contact with Rome. The location of these tribes, along the southern shores of England, would have offered up financial control of both imports and exports. To gain control of these tribes would have been essential for the expansion policies of the aggressive Catuvellauni tribe. The lands of the Regni tribe occupied east Sussex, south west Kent and, perhaps, included some of eastern Surrey. The Atrebates occupied the lands of Berkshire, Hampshire, parts of western Sussex, western Surrey and, perhaps, even into north east Wiltshire. As for the Belgae tribe, their lands seemed to incorporate modern Hampshire and parts of Avon/Somerset.

If we continue south west, we move into the lands of the Durotriges tribe, their lands incorporated southern Somerset and southern Wiltshire. They were bordered by the Belgae to the east and to the west by the

Dumnonii tribe. Historians suggest that the peoples of the Durotriges consisted of numerous independent factions, who eventually were subjugated by Vespasian and his 2nd Augusta Legion. The Dumnonii tribe could be found in Devon and Cornwall. These lands were important for the Romans as they contained valuable tin resources.

Casting an analytical eye upon the above paragraphs, it would be prudent to suggest that the most secure and safe region, at the time of the 43 AD invasion, was the southern coast. It was upon these shores I believe that the shadowy figure of Togidubnus (Cogidubnus), who has stalked his way through nearly 2,000 years of history, would have been welcomed. He could possibly have been escorted by the aging Verica. Later historians seem to have accepted that the name of Cogidubnus was, perhaps, an error of translation and copying of manuscripts and that the letter 'C' should have read as a 'T'. Therefore for the remainder of this chapter the name 'Togidubnus' will be used. More of this translation error can be read in 'The Minor Works of Tacitus', a study in textual criticism by Charles E Murgia.

THE DEVELOPING POLITICAL SITUATION

The future British king, Togidubnus, perhaps the son-in-law of Verica and, no doubt of royal birth, was chosen by Rome for possibly two reasons. He would have been accepted by the local tribe's ruling elite and, therefore, would not have been classed as a usurper. His education would have been streamlined on how to relate Romanisation and the process of Roman administration to the tribal elite of the Atrebates, the Belgae and the Regni. On a personal level, he would have been used to accommodation of some quality and comfort. I feel that he would not have arrived upon our British shores until the Fishbourne area was deemed secure. Perhaps then, Togidubnus would have been accompanied by the aging Verica sometime close to after 43 AD.

To the east of Fishbourne Roman Palace, excavations have revealed a series of timber buildings. No doubt some of these were related to the Roman Legions in 43 AD, as a supply/admin base. One of the timber buildings had 6-7 rooms and revealed itself as a building of significance. Three/four of this building's rooms may have been plastered white, with a white chalky mortar and painted red and white. It seems also to have contained a verandah and perhaps a colonnade of brick and stucco. Luxury indeed! – compared to the local living accommodation. I feel, close by, there would also have been accommodation for slaves to help and attend to this Royal Ambassador's everyday needs. The annals of history are relatively quiet about Togidubnus and, consequently, he becomes a rather phantom figure. His first names, Tiberius Claudius, are taken in honour of his patron the Emperor Claudius, although the name Togidubnus is of British origin. The Roman historian, Tacitus, tells us that 'certain states were presented to King Togidubnus, who maintained his unswerving loyalty right up to our own memory' (Tacitus, Agricola, 14). Could this statement be interpreted that Togidubnus was already in England at the time of the invasion?

If we flick through the pages of the history of Roman Britain, after 43 AD, and stop to view the period from around 60-80 AD, two major developments seem to engage thoughts and, consequently, stimulate interesting debate. After the Boudican uprising was extinguished by the Roman Governor Suetonius, the Roman Emperor Nero, perhaps somewhat traumatised by the violence and the near-loss of Britain as a province of the Roman Empire, decided on a policy of appeasement with a conciliatory approach towards the local tribes who were engaged in the rebellion. Consequently Gaius Suetonius Paulinus, Governor of Britain since 58 AD, with no doubt his emotions still raw at the carnage of death and destruction caused by Boudica's warriors, was withdrawn back to Rome. He was replaced by Publius Petronius Turpilianus (Governor of Britain from 62-63 AD). Nero's commands of appeasement, which included enhancing Roman culture in England, diplomacy and the encouragement of trade towards the tribes of Britannia, were consolidated with the appointment of Marcus Trebellius Maximus as Governor of England from 63-69 AD. Maximus pursued minimal martial activity; consequently, in 67 AD, the province seemed secure enough for the Legio XIV Gemina to withdraw from Britain and be deployed elsewhere, possibly in southern France. Maximus re-established Colchester (Camulodunm) but because of its vulnerability due to its geographical position, London (Londinium) was to become the new capital of England.

Due to Nero's death in 68 AD, civil war violently erupted in Italy and, in the time span of one year, Rome embraces four emperors (Galba, Otho, Aulus Vitellius Germanicus and Caesar Vespasianus Augustus). It was during this period of unrest that Maximus, Governor of Britain, was forced to flee for his life from Britain. Perhaps the Legions were unsettled by the unrest in Rome and their lack of military activity, compounded by their lack of bounty and possibly their low wages. Consequently Maxixmus, not being of a military background, seemed to have lost the Legion's respect. It has been suggested that during his flight one of his stopovers could have been Chedworth Roman Villa. This suggestion is offered up due to the discovery of a military intaglio found during the excavations of the villa.

Aulus Vitellius Germanicus, Roman Emperor from April-December 69 AD, replaced Maximus with Marcus Vettius Bolanus as Governor of Britain. When Vespasian was recognised by the Senate as the new Roman Emperor in December 69 AD, he allowed Bolanus to stay in office until 71 AD, when he was replaced by Quintus Petillius Cerialis. Also, Gnaeus Julius Agricola replaced Marcus Roscius Coeclius as commander of the Legio XX Valeria Victrix stationed in Britain. It seems then that Vespasian had made the decision that Britain was to remain an important province of the Roman Empire. Agricola's command ended in 73 AD, but he returned as Consul and Governor of Britain in 77 AD and completed Vespasian's expansive policies with the conquest of Wales and northern England. Agricola was eventually recalled to Rome in 87 AD by the Roman Emperor Domitian, a son of Vespasian. All this conquest was only possible as southern England had responded favourably to the foresight of the policies of Nero and, consequently, the Roman generals were never threatened by military unrest to their rear.

As the glowing embers of the Boudican rebellion began to fade, it becomes obvious from the above paragraphs that Nero was taking a 'gently, gently' approach towards the tribal elite of the defeated tribes and slowly, but carefully, encouraging them to recognise that prosperity is the bed-fellow of continuing peace. If we now turn our attention, during this same period of time, to the tribes of central and southern England, and especially at Fishbourne, Nero's fingerprints of encouraging the benefits of embracing Roman culture are perhaps more firmly recognised.

THE DEVELOPMENT OF FISHBOURNE

Opus Sectile flooring

Corinthian capital

At Fishbourne, after seven winters of excavations during the 1960s, the remains of a masonry building, christened with the name 'Proto-Palace', was released from its internment. Archaeology dates the structure of this building as being laid down between 60 and 70 AD. The Proto-Palace can be divided into four parts: to the north there is a courtyard surrounded by verandahs, to the south there is a bath suite and along the east side of both is a range of rooms flanked by corridors. It is possible that there was another range of rooms to the south west. All was built on virgin ground. Its total area covered 2,300 square metres/25,000 square feet in area. Also revealed by archaeologists, during those seven winters, as their inquisitive trowels picked their way through many tons of earth, were the imprints of a posse of Mediterranean artisans. The craftsmanship of masons and sculptors were recognised with the discovery of parts of Corinthian columns which were composed of oolitic limestone, with capitals on fluted stuccoed shafts. Also detected were the fingerprints of mosaisists with the finding of small parts of black and white mosaics and opus sectile flooring. The handiwork of marble workers and stucco craftsmen were also recognised. Numerous pieces of painted wall-plaster, which embraced the talents of the painters, showed the enormous variety and skill of their work. Foliage and floral designs and panels, decorated in many colours, including red, blue, green, white and various shades of pink, were excavated. Other designs were painted in blue/black, yellow and red. These bold, clear colours were outlined with a white frame. The construction of this whole building would have needed the considerable experience of a Mediterranean architect.

Could it be, then, that this sophisticated, elegant and architecturally unique home, for this period in time, was a gift of gratitude to Togidubnus from the Roman Emperor Nero for keeping his tribesmen from any detrimental involvement with the Boudican uprising? Through the acceptance of this gift from Nero, Togidubnus becomes an ambassador of Roman culture and, consequently, his tribal elite and wealthy entrepreneurs commission the building of their own 'villas' along the coast of Sussex and Hampshire. Villas have been recognised through archaeological excavations at Angmering, Pulborough and Southwick. Although, the other alternative is that Togidubnus' loyalty to Rome was not tested, as his lands were never threatened by the Boudican uprising, as they were geographically too far to the south west. Therefore, Togidubnus, with his increasing financial prosperity, may have commissioned construction of the Proto-Palace himself.

After the death of Nero in 68 AD Vespasian, the first Emperor of the Flavian dynasty, continues the policy of encouraging Roman culture and the acceptance, and therefore the benefits, of Roman administration to the conquered tribes of this imperial province. This policy reached its pinnacle when civitas (city/town council) were established in each tribal capital. Certain council members were held directly responsible to the provincial governor for the efficient administration of the region. It seems that the tribal elite were the ones commissioned into these administrative positions. Tribal capitals were established within the conquered tribes, one in each of the tribal regions. Seventeen of these tribal capitals had their tribal name incorporated into the name of the city. For example, the Atrebates tribal civitas (now Silchester) was Calleva

Atrebatum and the Dubunni tribal civitas (now Cirencester) was named Corinium Dobunnorum.

Turning our attention back to the Fishbourne area and with our eyes focused to the west, a new masonry building was begun. Dwarfing in scale the Proto-Palace, it was being built possibly to replace it, but the construction was never finished. The ground-plan of this building is incompletely known as the mosaic floors of the later Flavian palace prevented excavation down to the earlier surface, and the building extends beyond the south and west limits of the available site. The surviving fragments, which were excavated in the 1960s, are of the north-west corner of this structure. I wonder then, what unexpected situation developed to cause the decision to be taken to abort this build? Two possible scenarios begin to fester up in my thoughts and both involve the hand of the Emperor Vespasian. But of course there are, no doubt, other explanations that as yet my mind is not conscious of. I decide to seek out the bust of Vespasian from within the Flavian Palace museum and as my eyes

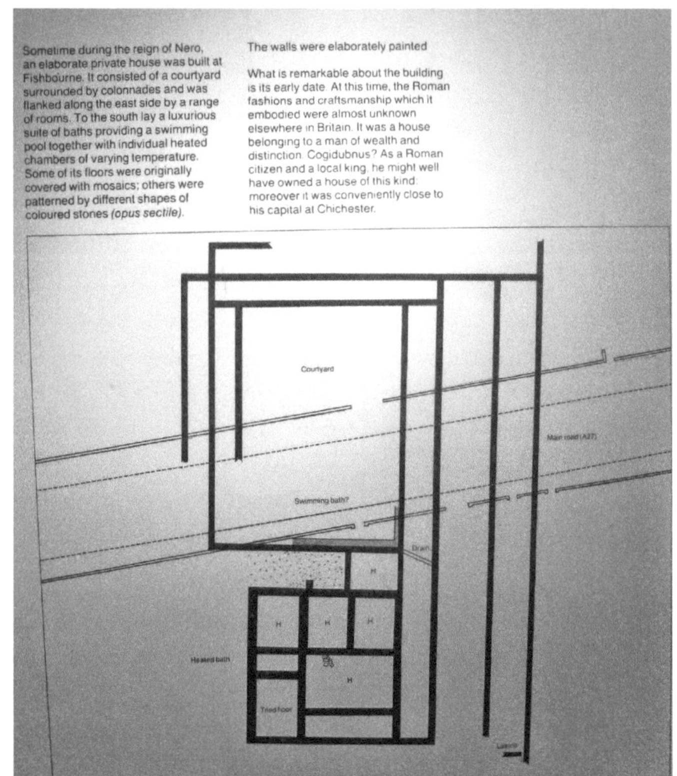

Plan of the Proto-Palace

absorb his solid facial features, my imagination immediately conjures up a man in possession of a lively and adventurous spirit – but, being a man of a military background, he would have been aware of his own mortality. Consequently, after investing and spending money on the restoration of Rome, after the civil war, with a new forum and public works which included an upgrade of the public baths, he embarks on a series of classical building projects. These included the construction of the Flavian amphitheatre, known today as the Colosseum/Coliseum, the Temple of Peace and the Temple to the defied Claudius. In 75 AD he erected – although this was begun under Nero – a colossal statue of Apollo. Vespasian, no doubt, realised these projects would enhance his legacy as a worthy emperor and servant of Rome and his memory would be 'engraved in stone' for many centuries in the foreseeable future. Vespasian, with his mind at peace with the plans laid out for the rebirth of Rome after the destruction of the civil war, turned his eyes to the north and took an inquisitive look at the Imperial Province of Britannia.

TOGIDUBNUS AND FISHBOURNE

The original inscripition   *The reconstructed inscripition*

In 1723 the ghost of Togidubnus/Cogidubnus appears again, this time on a piece of Purbeck marble which was found when a cellar was being constructed on the corner of North Street and Lion Street, in Chichester. The left hand portion of it was missing and during its recovery it was broken into four pieces. Sadly, its repair using cement was of poor workmanship. The fifth line of the inscription on this marble tablet seems to have presented historians and archaeologists a problem with interpretation of its true meaning. At the time of its discovery it was interpreted to read that Togidubnus was granted the title of 'Legatus Augusti' (Imperial Legate in Britain). The alternative interpretation suggests that Togidubnus became not an 'Imperial Legate', but 'Great King in Britain'. This alternative and later interpretation came to light when the inscription was re-examined by Professor Bogaers of Nijmegen University, in 1979.

The inscription can be dated to the 1st century AD by the appearance on it of the name 'Togidubnus' (Cogidubnus). But who the Emperor was at the time of the laying down of this slab is ambiguous, as Togidubnus could have lived through the reigns of the following Emperors: from 41-54 AD it was Claudius; from 54-68 AD – Nero; from 69-79 AD – Vespasian; from 79-81 AD – Titus; and lastly from 81-96 AD - Domitian. Sadly, it seems that the death of Togidubnus went unrecorded and also, unfortunately, this man's age is unknown when the Roman invasion of Britannia took place in 43 AD.

The original interpretation of the inscription, in 1723, of bestowing Togidubnus as 'Legatus Augisti' (envoy of the Emperor) would have made Togidubnus, as an imperial Legate, eligible to occupy a seat in the Roman Senate. The giving of this title to Togidubnus was conceived by the early historians to be within the reign of the Emperor Vespasian. This assumption raises a number of debateable scenarios. The bestowing of this title to a client king of an Imperial province would have been unique as the receiver would usually be a General in the Roman army, and the men who filled this office as legate were drawn from the senatorial class of Rome. The post was generally appointed by the Emperor and its receiver was usually a former Tribune (military).

Taking a practical view, if indeed Vespasian did bestow this honour upon Togidubnus, as head of provincial administration and chief judicial officer of the province, but subservient to the authority of Agricola (Consul and Governor of Britannia, 77-85 AD), it would have been of great benefit to Agricola himself. Gnaeus Julius Agricola's military plate was full. The Ordovices tribe of north Wales needed to be subjugated, as did the Island Mona (Anglesey). Agricola expanded his military might into Caledonia (Scotland) and needed to fortify the coast facing Ireland. There would have been a huge development of Imperial administration and of local government within these provinces, and the experience of Togidubnus would have been invaluable. Although his appointment would have been viewed by many as socially unacceptable, Rome was in effect being run by a military dictatorship, and this appointment could have been recognised as Vespasian displaying great vision and power for the continuation of the Romanisation of Britannia.

Then, in 1979, Professor J E Bogaers published an article in Volume 10 of Britannia under the heading 'King Cogidubnus in Chichester: another reading of RIB 91' which interpreted line 5 of the inscription as reading 'Cogidubnus Great King in Britain'. His interpretation seems to have been accepted by historians and academics as the true reading and meaning of the inscription.

If we accept that Togidubnus was never elevated to the rank of Legatus Augusti, we must search for other explanations as to why the splendours of the garden and the dignified and cultured architecture were laid down at Fishbourne. Consequently my mind becomes a flowering bush of possibilities – each stem leading and then growing in a different direction.

WHAT WAS FISHBOURNE ROMAN PALACE?

Vespasian

Mosaic comparisons to those found in Italy

The question that now has to be confronted is – what evidence is available to be able to date the construction of this magnificent building which covered an area, including its gardens, of at least 10 acres? Eighty-six coins were recovered from the site during the 1960s excavations; the latest coins were of a Vespasian issue and dated to 73 AD. This possibly suggests that the erection of the palace began soon after this date. Sherds of decorated samian vessels, excavated on site, were dated within the range of 70-85 AD. Some were comparable to vessels that were excavated at the town of Pompeii (near modern Naples).

In 79 AD, the volcano known as Vesuvius vomited up fire, death and destruction in the form of a pyroclastic flow, a fluidised mass of rock fragments and gases which buried Pompeii (and Herculaneum) beneath layers of ash and pumice to a depth of 4-6 metres (13-20 feet).Pompeii was frozen in time until it was discovered in

1748. Intriguingly, a number of black and white geometric mosaics were discovered during the excavations at Pompeii and at Herculaneum. These mosaics were strikingly similar to those found within the North and West wings of Fishbourne Roman Palace. These similarities in style, perhaps, suggest that these black and white mosaic floor designs were the fashion of the time and can help support the dating of the build at Fishbourne to within a start date of 73 AD, with the finishing touches of the layout of the Flavian garden at about 80 AD.

THE PALACE TAKES SHAPE

The palace at Fishbourne incorporated the most up-to-date ideas in Roman architecture. The gardens and courtyards were surrounded by wide colonnaded walks in the Hellenistic style which was becoming popular in Rome at the time.

In the centre of the west wing was a vaulted Audience Chamber approached by a flight of steps from the garden.
In here, the owner would have met important visitors.

The palace was entered through a large Entrance Hall at the centre of the East Wing. It had a marble lined pool at its inner end. The shape of the Hall and pool is probably based on the old Roman idea of an atrium with an impluvium, seen frequently in the houses of Pompeii. However, at Fishbourne the design has been modified to suit the current fashion.

Front of the Audience Chamber

The Entrance Hall seen from the formal garden

Once again my thoughts are drawn towards the hands and mind of Vespasian as being responsible for aborting the build of the second masonry building at Fishbourne and, consequently, sowing the seed that would eventually germinate and flourish to become the largest classical establishment, as yet discovered, north of the Alps and become known as Fishbourne Roman Palace. Vespasian, with his legacy of building in Rome, that would hold his name secure in the country of his birth, was perhaps not satisfied – this astute Emperor also wanted to leave a lasting memory of his rule in the furthest outpost of the Roman Empire, Britannia.

What followed was possibly a consultation, perhaps in Rome, between Vespasian, Togidubnus and Vespasian's chosen architect. They would have engaged together on the composition and utilisation of the newly planned construction. It would, therefore, be appropriate if we now delve into excavation reports of the 1960s and take an inquisitive view of the design and ground plan of the individual wings of the Palace.

WEST WING AND MOSAICS

You are standing above the remains of the northern part of the west wing of the Palace, which stretched from the modern building in front of you, under your feet, to the main road behind you. The fence to your left stands just beyond the line of the west wall of a long corridor which ran along the length of the west wing. The remains of the apse at its northern end may be seen inside the audio-visual theatre in front of you. Five damaged mosaics were found in this area during the 1960s but were reburied for their protection.

The Palace consisted of three self-contained ranges — north, east and south wings, each with their own courtyards/terraces. But it was the West Wing which, on entry to the Palace grounds through the grand Entrance Hall, would have engulfed the visitors' visual mind and demanded their immediate attention. Standing five feet higher than the other wings it dominated the skyline. In the centre of this wing was a square room with an apsidal recess opening out of its west wall which Barry Cunliffe christened as an Audience Chamber. This chamber, it seems, had a mosaic floor which included tesserae of white, black, yellow and red. The size of the tesserae were 3/16th of an inch in size (0.5cm). This suggests that this floor was of high-class craftsmanship. Perhaps lining the apse was a timber bench, no doubt decorated with the finest silk cloth. The vaulted ceiling was dressed with the colours of white ribs against the background of bright blue, purple and red. This would have given the impression to the visitor that the person seated upon the bench would be like a god within the heavens. One can imagine that the Rex Magus (Great King in Britain) Togidubnus would have received visiting dignitaries within this chamber. How many rooms existed within

ENTRANCE HALL

You are standing over the remains of the entrance hall, a very large building, 13.5m wide by almost 30m long. Inside, it was divided by two cross-walls, each pierced by three arched openings through which the wide central passage ran.
On either side, five rooms opened onto this passage.
Behind you, the modern concrete tank marks the position of a marble-lined pool and fountain.
There would have been large porticos at either end of the hall comprising six columns supporting a triangular pediment.
It would have been an appropriately grand entrance for a grand Palace.

this west range is unknown, although many/all would have been paved with mosaic floors. Parts of three floors were lifted and are on display in the North Wing of the Palace; others were reburied for posterity. The Audience Chamber was isolated from these adjacent rooms by side corridors. It has been suggested that the rooms beyond would have been utilised as state rooms/suites. Beyond these was a western corridor running the full length of the wing and close to its northern apse, modern-day visitors can view an audio-visual film, documenting the rise and fall of the Palace. This corridor was void of a mosaic pavement but was blessed with painted wall-plaster. In all probability it was a hippodromos (an area for casual exercise).

This wing could possibly also have been used as an administrative centre of learning for the sons of the tribal elite, for the legal aspects of Roman administration were complex and numerous sensitive issues regarding individual tribal customs could make the assimilation of Roman law far from straightforward. This is perhaps confirmed by visits to Britain from high-regarded lawyers/jurists, such as – Salvius,

AUDIENCE CHAMBER AND STATUE BASE

The steps in front of you mark the position of the original flight of steps leading up to the audience chamber. This chamber was 10.7m wide by 9.4m deep with a semi-circular apse, 6.1m diameter, set into its far wall. It would have been the focal point of the whole Palace, and it may have been from here that Tiberius Claudius Togidubnus ruled his kingdom. At your feet is a square of stone and tile. This was probabl the base of a statue, possibly a statue of the Emperor.

Liberalis and Iavolenus Priscus. Latin could have been taught here and much could be learned from lectures in Roman history and mythology.

The South Wing, with its principal aspect to the south, was constructed with a terraced garden stretching a distance of 350 feet (106 metres) south from the building to the estuary beyond. It has been assumed that this wing with its range of rooms would have been the residence of Togidubnus and his immediate family – all were served with the luxury of a close-by bath suite. Invited dignitaries could have enjoyed sharing a meal with the Royal Family with the added visual bonus of a sea view. Sadly, most of this wing is interred beneath the main A259 road and the houses and gardens that line its southern side. It can be assumed that most, if not all, rooms would have been paved with mosaics and with high class interior décor. In 1805, a black and white mosaic pavement, 13.5 feet (4.1 metres) wide was noticed during building work in the village, close to the main road.

EAST WING

The paving slabs set in the grass show the position of the walls of part of the Palace's east wing. This area, between the aisled hall to your left, and the entrance hall to your right, was taken up by a range of rooms and two courtyards or gardens, partially surrounded by colonnades.
The east wing continued to the south of the entrance hall but much of it is now beneath the modern buildings and the road. The main Palace baths were located at the southern end of this wing.

During its heyday the Roman Palace may have accommodated at least 70 mosaic floors. Today some of their remains congregate within the North Wing under its cover building. Waiting to be viewed by the modern visitors is a collection of black and white geometric and polychrome mosaics. The black and white geometric mosaics are predominately the 1st century floors of the North Wing although the 'Small Cross and Box' Mosaic is late 2nd century. This possibly suggests that black and white geometric designs were still popular at this time. Only one polychrome mosaic was dated to the 1st century and survives under the title 'Floral Mosaic', in Room 20. The other colourful floors were laid at a later period during the life of the Palace. The 'Knot' Mosaic was dated to the early 3rd century. Within the 2nd century the 'Shell' Mosaic, 'Greek key and Medusa' Mosaic and the most popular and well-known mosaic today, 'Cupid on a Dolphin', were crafted. Interestingly, this mosaic floor was lifted for conservation purposes in 1987 and beneath it appeared the 'Fortress' Mosaic, which can now be viewed further down the wing. Also within the 2nd century the North Wing and the West Wing were connected by the laying down of a mosaic corridor.

AISLED HALL

This was a large room with a roof supported partly on its sid[e] walls and partly on two rows of four piers. The foundations were strengthened by wooden piles to take the weight of such a large structure. It is not known what the building wa[s] used for, but there would have been space for a large number of people. At some time after AD 100 the building was reduced in width and the colonnade removed from its eastern end. This smaller building probably became the exercise hall for the adjoining bath suite, behind you.

The North Wing was concluded to be a residential range of rooms. Most prominent were two suites of rooms with their own private colonnaded courtyards. These courtyards, laid out with shrubs and flowers, would have created a relaxing, peaceful and personal atmosphere. The archaeology suggests that these two ranges of rooms were cut off from the main communal formal garden to the south.

It is the East Wing which would have engulfed most of the earlier Proto-Palace that stood to the south of the Entrance Hall. It is within this area that the Bath Suite, although possibly altered in some parts of its original construction, would have continued in use. It is probable that a range of rooms would have been added to the older ones of the Proto-Palace, perhaps to balance up architecturally the known range of 11 rooms to the north of the Entrance Hall. The northern side of the Entrance Hall contained two colonnaded courtyards, both probably embellished with bushes, shrubs and with climbing plants to decorate the bare walls, and to the east of these courtyards stood the range of rooms. It is possible that a narrow colonnaded courtyard existed to the south of the Entrance Hall to help retain the necessary symmetry of the East Wing. At the extreme northern end of this wing stood a building, known as the Aisled Hall, which measured internally 88 by 66 feet (26.7 by 20 metres). This massive structure of classical architecture reflects a hall of some significance. Although the excavations of the 1960s failed to confirm the presence of any mosaic flooring, quantities of painted wall-plaster were recognised, mostly of plain red and white; other pieces embraced grey/black, yellow, pink and streaky green.

The Roman name for Chichester was Noviomagus Regnensium and it was seemingly expanding with its civil development during the construction of the Palace. Around 80 AD an amphitheatre was built, capable of seating 800 people, at what is now known as Eastgate. Today, in Tower Road and in situ within the Novium Museum, are the remains of a Roman bath-house. Today Chichester acknowledges its Roman past with four plaques set in pavements carrying the name Noviomagus Reginorum, perhaps meaning 'the new town/market of the proud people'. These plaques are laid close to the sites of the town's four Roman gates, one each in North Street, East Street, South Street and West Street.

The port at Fishbourne would have been constantly busy with imports for the Romano-British inhabitants. A range of luxury goods including elegant glass vessels and pottery lamps would have been flooding in from Italy and Gaul. Galleys would have brought in amphorae, made and filled in Southern Spain, some containing wine, but most containing olive oil or fish products. The cross-Channel trade would also have brought in fine tableware (samian) and various kinds of attractive jewellery. The exports from Fishbourne would have included grain, cattle, hunting dogs and iron. It is possible that the range of rooms on the northern side of the East Wing could have been utilised by the businessmen involved in importing and exporting, for wining and dining and concluding lucrative deals.

Tax collectors would possibly have inhabited the Aisled Hall, not just dealing with the business of the port but also administering local taxes for the benefit of the growth of Noviomagus Regnensium. This huge building could have served the local population as the main administrative centre, dealing with legal disputes and people accused of criminal offences. It has been suggested that there may have been a shrine within this building and it is possible that the Iron Age Temple on Hayling Island, 15 miles to the west, was refurbished during this period of expansion. It seems that this Aisled Hall could only be accessed from outside the Palace grounds.

THE ROMAN GARDENS

The four wings of the Palace enclosed an area of 258 by 320 feet (78.4 by 97.6 metres), laid out as a formal garden with a number of features incorporated into its design. The garden had a central pathway which

FORMAL GARDEN

Guide Book

The formal garden that you see in front of you was planted in the mid 1960s to recreate the first-century formal garden. The hedges were planted along the lines of bedding trenches discovered during archaeological excavations. Box *(Buxus sempervirens)* was chosen for replanting the hedges as there is literary evidence for the Romans having used it in this way. The original garden was twice the size of this one. The southern half lies beneath the private houses and gardens and was probably a mirror image of this northern half.

was 40 feet (12.2 metres) wide, running the full length of the garden from the Entrance Hall (east) to the Audience Chamber (west).Today only the northern half of the garden survives as the southern half lies beneath the modern road and houses. This sophisticated visual culture ushered in the thrilling power of classical architecture combined with a stylized garden. The garden would have been supplied with piped water serving ornamental basins and fountains which were set around the pathways. These basins/fountains would have been displayed against the inner hedgerows, although the spurt of water into the air from the fountains would have been no more than three to four feet. Other garden décor may have included stone/marble statues, perhaps of selected Roman deities. The base of a possible statue can be viewed close to the West Wing. The viewing concept of the garden would have been paramount in the mind of its designer,

THE WEST WING TERRACE

Revetment Wall, Gully, Tank Base and Column Bases

To your right is the revetment wall that supported the front of the west wing terrace and was originally plastered, and painted with leaves and flowers. In front of it is a drainage gully, made from massive stone blocks, which carried away rainwater. The stone walls near the hedge are all that remain of a water storage tank. Water would have flowed from it through ceramic pipes to fountains in the garden and entrance hall. The two surviving column bases are important as they show the distance between the columns that once surrounded the garden.

therefore not to detract from this, the external face of the West Wing wall was plastered and then painted with a dark-green background against which boldly drawn foliage was set. To the upper-class visitor from Italy these gardens would have been no more than a peaceful place to amble round while chatting with their friends, but to the local population of the expanding town these gardens would have been unique.

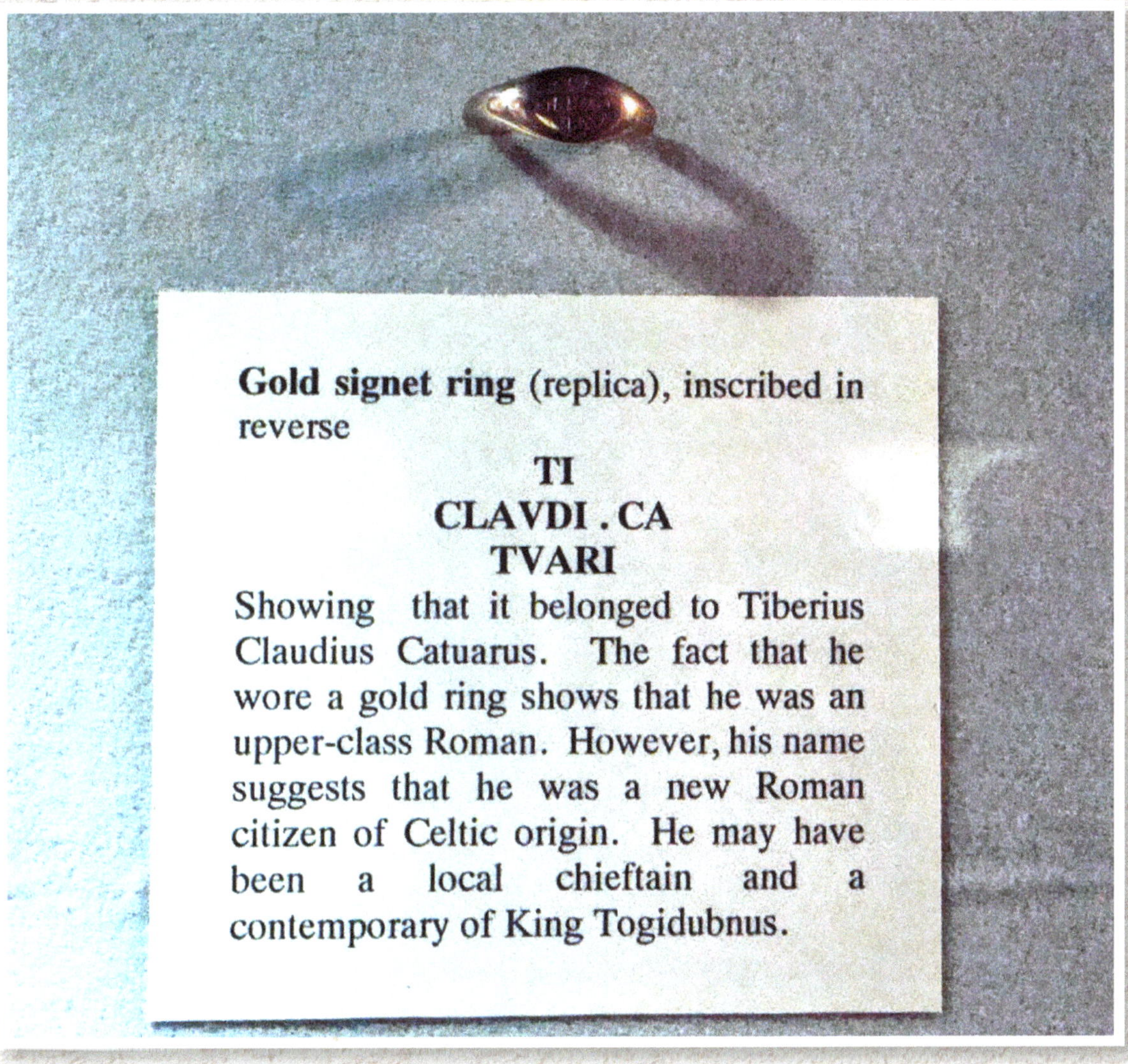

Gold signet ring (replica), inscribed in reverse

**TI
CLAVDI . CA
TVARI**

Showing that it belonged to Tiberius Claudius Catuarus. The fact that he wore a gold ring shows that he was an upper-class Roman. However, his name suggests that he was a new Roman citizen of Celtic origin. He may have been a local chieftain and a contemporary of King Togidubnus.

Gold Signet Ring

CONCLUSION

If indeed King Togidubnus did reside here, on his death all his territory would have been incorporated into the province, and possibly sold. Perhaps it was purchased by Tiberius Claudius Catuarus – his personal finger-ring was discovered beyond the Palace grounds to the east. A replica is on display in the Palace Museum. This classical building survived, although reduced in size, for over two hundred years. In its final form it was properly an impressive, comfortable and stylish villa. A new bath suite was constructed in the corridor between the North Wing and the Aisled Hall. Some of the rooms were redesigned and redecorated, and several of the geometric black and white mosaics of the first century were replaced by the more colourful polychrome mosaics which can be viewed today. Around 280-290 AD the sun finally set on Fishbourne Roman Palace when it was felled by the power of fire. It destroyed much of the North Wing and possibly the northern side of the West Wing, leaving only the stone walls standing. These stone walls were systematically robbed away to be used as building material elsewhere. The church in Fishbourne carries some of the Palace remains .Stone robbing was still in practice during the thirteenth/fourteenth century as the medieval farmers discovered the Roman flint footings across the West Wing. In due course the fields were turned over to pasture, creating 9-12 inches (0.2-0.3 metres) of top soil. So it came to pass that the Palace remains were undisturbed, until they were resurrected one April day in 1960, when the mouth of a mechanical digger chewed up and spat out a combination of mosaic flooring and Roman building material during the construction of a trench for the laying out of a water main. Consequently, in late August of 1968 the Palace remains were laid out for public viewing. For many months queues of visitors waited patiently to feast their eyes on some of the very first Roman mosaic floors laid down in the Imperial Province of Britannia.

Chapter III

TOUR AND DISCUSSION OF THE
FISHBOURNE ROMAN PALACE MOSAICS

Fishbourne Roman Palace

AN OVERVIEW

Many thousands of years ago, somewhere, perhaps on a sandy beach, a young child makes a face of his mother, father or younger sibling, using a pile of varying shaped and coloured pebbles gathered together from the shores of the beach. Excitedly, the child calls to his parents to come and view his efforts before the in-coming tide destroys his creation. The parents praise the child's efforts and, suitably encouraged, the child returns to the beach at a later date with friends and they all begin to make images in the sand with the pebbles. Perhaps competitions are arranged and families have beach parties when the children's efforts are shown, discussed and judged. Over the course of time this child grows up and with practised skills learned from the beach, wishes to make one of their creations more permanent.

These humble beginnings of human imagination and skills, lead eventually to the creation of the mosaic floors which many of us enjoy today. The materials used over time progressed from coloured pebbles to natural coloured stone, now known as tesserae. The tesserae in Britain range in size from 0.5cm to 4cm and are usually sourced from the local natural stone.

The architect Vitruvius, in the first century BC, tells us that a sound base for the mosaic to rest in was most important. He goes on to say that the soil should be levelled and rubble, mixed with lime, should be rammed tightly down. Upon this a layer of powdered pottery mixed with lime should be used to create the bedding for the mosaic. This should then be covered with a fine layer of mortar in which to lay the tesserae.

There seems to be very little historical evidence of whom these craftsmen were and the methods they employed to create and lay their mosaics. By the time mosaics were laid in Britain the art was many centuries old. Many modern mosaicists use, what is called, 'the reverse' method or the 'indirect' method – both linked to what is known as prefabrication. Whether these methods were used by the ancient craftsmen are open to debate as no known proof is available.

What I am trying to encourage through this chapter is for visitors, not just to view mosaics with their eyes just as works of art, but also to open their minds and imaginations to what, perhaps, these mosaics may be trying to tell us.

The first mosaic to view is to the right, just past the model in the foyer. It is a mosaic corridor created in the 2nd century to link the North Wing to the West Wing. Looking at it now, damaged by blistering and agriculture, it is difficult to see the original design. But it consisted of 22 alternating red and grey boxes, each box containing diagonal crosses made up of nine smaller boxes of grey and red, the red being made of recycled tile and the grey possibly Kimmeridge shale, from Dorset. The pattern of this floor becomes much clearer when delicately moistened with a damp mop.

Next on the left is the 'Nine Squared Mosaic and Hypocaust'. Towards the end of the 3rd century AD, around the year 270 AD, this hypocaust was constructed but never used. The floor level was going to be raised and in all probability a new mosaic floor would have been laid. This is indicated by the discovery, in the room opposite, of two heaps of gritty mortar already mixed and ready for use. Upturned roof tiles were used for the floors and the side walls were built of greensand blocks with bonding courses of tile set in clay. To the far right, part of the original mosaic floor can be seen. This is a complex mosaic floor consisting of a geometric pattern of squares within squares. There are black lines on a white background and a limited use of red and blue/grey colours. The white tesserae are chalk, the black is possibly shale, the red is a baked clay and the grey is lias limestone.

If we progress down the North Wing, the next room to our right is the 'Square and Diamond Pattern' mosaic. The floor is basically white with a design of evenly spaced boxes linked by a square and diamond pattern. The boxes contain one of three designs, based on squares: a black square, a white square within a larger black one and a third is a motif containing five white squares. In part, the floor has subsided over an earlier ditch and the resulting rising damp would have made the room perhaps unsuitable for everyday living. Consequently, the room could well have been used as a store or workshop. This could explain why the mosaic was left undisturbed and not refurbished as other rooms had been during later developments. The tesserae would have been made of a hard white chalk and a grey/black hard silty shale.

The next room on the right hand side carries the heading 'Chequerboard' mosaic. Some of the original mosaic laid down between AD 73-80 can be seen in the south west and north east corners. The mosaic consists of a repetitive design of black squares of two different sizes, on a white ground. These boxes are contained within a triple black border. This room, like the previous room, probably became a workshop of some design. The tesserae are made out of white chalk and a grey/black silty shale.

If we cast our eyes to the left, we see a room known as the 'Shell Mosaic'. This mosaic is dated by the shards of broken samian pottery used as tesserae, therefore it is believed to have been constructed in the middle of the 2nd century AD. Materials used for the construction of the 2nd century mosaic include samian pottery, red tile for the border, a hard white chalk and a yellow siltstone, in all probability from Dorset. Some of the red tesserae could have been made from red brick. The design of this mosaic, because of its missing centre piece, is difficult to interpret. The semicircles of ray panels, on the north and south side, could be scallop shells. Alternatively, the long narrow pieces of mosaic protruding from the bottom of the missing centre, could be interpreted as the legs, feet and spurs of a peacock. The 'shells' could then be interpreted as the opened tail of a peacock. In the late 1960s when this mosaic was being consolidated by two Italian craftsmen, they referred to this floor as the 'Peacock Mosaic'. The symbolism of the peacock can be open to a number of interpretations. The Ancient Greeks likened the peacock tail to stars, or to eyes, and dedicated this bird to Juno the Goddess of sky and the Goddess of stars, and souls through the peacock were raised to the bosom of Juno, a place where souls migrated therefore symbolising immortality. The Christians in antiquity used the symbolism of the peacock as resurrection. The circular shape of the peacock tail gives the interpretation of immortality and eternity. On reflection, and in all probability, one could see this as a scallop shell with two dangling tails of dolphins. A marine scene on this floor would not have been out of place, for the palace itself is very close to the sea. In all probability, the centre of this mosaic was destroyed by the roots of a tree.

To our left we can now view the mosaic named 'Cupid on a Dolphin'. This is the most famous and the most colourful of the Fishbourne mosaics and has been seen on a number of television documentaries. The tesserae used to construct this piece of work include yellow and orange limestone and ceramic fragments, including shards of samian pottery, which are recognisable by their bright reddish/orange colour. Chalk and grey shale were also used in its construction. This mosaic is believed to have been crafted between AD 150-160. The evidence for this was found when the mosaic was lifted for conservation in 1979 – the samian pottery used for the tesserae were dated to that period by the patterned design on the reverse side. The mosaic is 13 feet square and contains several images that relate to Greek/Roman mythology. A discussion on this mosaic can be viewed under the heading 'Cupid on a Dolphin'. Interestingly, a small black bird is to be seen perched on the third leaf west from the central vase in the northern border. Is this the signature of the mosaicist?

Next on the left, past 'Cupid on a Dolphin', is a room which carries the heading 'The Knot Mosaic'. The mosaic panel of this room is 7'4" by 5'6" and the floor probably dates to the early 3rd century. For, during excavation nearby, underneath the tessellated floor, a silver coin of Septimius Severus, minted in 197 AD, was found. The material used for the tesserae in this room included chalk, shale, black pot, red brick, a yellow siltstone and a little samian. On the outside of the guilloche, on the white background, four pairs of dolphins can be seen, each pair facing a central vase. At this point I would like to give the reader a personal interpretation of this mosaic. The centre motif of this mosaic, the Solomon knot, has no visible beginning or end and could be read as immortality and eternity intertwined. Beliefs in that period of time, about what happened to the human spirit after death, would recognise this. In Roman literature, art and statuary the dolphin carries souls to the 'Island of the Blest'. Images of dolphins have been found in the hands of the dead to ensure safe passage to the afterlife. Dolphins were seen to be the travellers between the two worlds. They shared the human world by breathing air and showed intelligence and friendship towards humans. Then they could simply disappear to the unknown world beneath the waves, becoming a symbol of the renewal and preservation of life. The central motif is surrounded by never ending braided guilloche which could act as the demon trap to protect this motif from contamination (refer to 'Cupid on a Dolphin' below). The four vases between the dolphins could represent water, and the scallop shells, in the four corners of the mosaic, could represent food from the sea, as food and water are required for human existence. Alternatively, the

Solomon knot could represent the coming together of the Celtic culture with the Roman culture. The Roman culture would have been spreading through the country since AD 43 and by the 3rd century AD the two cultures would have become more integrated.

The next room to view is called the 'Doormat Mosaic and Burial'. Only a small part of the original mosaic survives which is in the south east corner. It shows a black chequer pattern on a white background, enclosed by a thin black line. This piece of mosaic could be a part of what is called a 'mat', this being the first part of the floor before leading on to the main mosaic. Again we have chalk used for the white tesserae and shale for the thin black line.

If we now continue down the North Wing we can view the 'Rosette and Tessellated Floor'. Fortunately, the mosaic, over a long period of time, has subsided into an underlying gully, thus saving it from complete destruction by the plough. It has been difficult to date this mosaic for although some of the tesserae are of samian pot, it has been impossible to date them. Therefore, all that can be said is that this floor would have been crafted after the beginning of the 2nd century. The mosaic panel is 6'9" square and the multi-coloured piece of work rests in the centre of a red tessellated floor. The rose was unknown to the inhabitants of Italy until the 3rd century BC, and the Latin name for the plant derives from its Greek name. The rose in its everyday and symbolic use in all probability was the result of a cultural contact with the Greeks, therefore we could read this rosette, by the time this mosaic was crafted, as the coming together of the Greek/Roman and Celtic cultures. The border design surrounding the whole mosaic could possibly be small rose leaves connected together by a continuous undulating pattern between the leaves.

Opposite this room we can view the 'Fortress' mosaic. This Flavian mosaic was found in 1987 when the 'Dolphin Mosaic' above it was lifted for restoration. This mosaic can also be viewed at ground level from the lower concourse. The outer border of this mosaic depicts a castellated city wall, an entry to within it is protected by gates in the middle of each wall with viewing towers in the four corners. There are two double portal in the middle of the north and south walls and two single portal in the middle of the east and west walls. The gates and the towers are enlivened with the use of grey and red tesserae. The central panel of this mosaic would have contained 16 equal squares, although sadly only nine survive, and some of these only contain fragments. They seem to be based on an intricate geometric design containing squares and triangles. The materials used for the construction include red ceramics, pale grey limestone, chalk and cement stone. If, in our mind's eye, we transport this mosaic back to the room where the Cupid on a Dolphin Mosaic is, we can then see this as a possible dining room with the colonnaded courtyard to the south of it. Perhaps the symbolism of this room is that the great wealth of the proprietor and his family protected them from the reality and complications of everyday life. With the dining couches positioned around the city walls, the diners could observe and discuss the 16 inner squares, splendidly laid out with their complicated and visually interesting designs. The craftsman/men who laid this mosaic would have been highly skilled and possibly well paid. They would also be aware that the design of this floor would abide in the visitors' visual memories, and in this way, perhaps, be relayed back to Rome as one of the more splendid rooms at that huge villa on the outskirts of Noviomagus Regnensium.

Alternatively, this mosaic could be viewed as an early street layout of Chichester. The locals, in all probability, would have known this place as Noviomagus Reginorum, meaning 'the new town - or market, of the proud people'. The mosaic depicts a north, east, south and west gate. Four roads radiate from Noviomagus. Outside the north gate a road goes to Calleva Atrebatum (Silchester), the capital of the Northern Atrebates. The road issuing from the east gate is Stane Street and goes to Londinium (London). From the south gate the road would have run to Selsey, on the coast. The road from the west gate went to Clausentum (Bitterne, Southampton).

Now we backtrack to the room which is called the 'Large Cross and Box' mosaic. In the Flavian period the wall plaster in this room was very elaborately painted, with large areas of simulated marble veneering of different types, perhaps indicating that this was a dining room. This mosaic was only 18 inches below the surface when found, and the only damage to it seems to be just ordinary wear and tear, as small areas in the north and south panels have been patched. The crosses and boxes are linked with a square-and-diamond background, cleverly designed to tantalise and tease our eyes as we search to seek and make visual sense of the design. Sometimes when I view this mosaic floor I feel that I am drowning in my own shadow, as I constantly feel that the watchful eyes of the past laid this mosaic with some meaning. This floor certainly stimulates my imagination and in my mind's eye I can see this mosaic being utilised as a chequer board game – the players, relaxing on their couches, sipping wine and getting the slaves to move their counters around the floor. Chalk and shale are the components of this floor. At a later date this floor was divided by a timber wall and, sadly, this partly destroys the whole visual perspective.

The next floor we come to is the 'Greek Key and Medusa' mosaic. This colourful mosaic and the original floor underneath it were both lifted and relayed for conservation purposes in 1981. A piece of the original black and white geometric mosaic can be seen in the south east corner of the floor. This fragment shows a meander pattern which would have surrounded squares containing geometric designs. Large areas of the original mosaic have been used to supplement the material used for the later floor. The material used in the later floor contains a wide tapestry of colour. Reds can be seen in siltstone, brick and samian. A yellow siltstone and its purple tones can also be noticed. Purple is also present in the form of Purbeck marble within the Medusa head and guilloche. The black/grey colours are of shale, although some of the grey is lias limestone with the occasional use of flint. The pieces of samian date this floor as being laid at the beginning of the 2nd century. The decorated panel measures 13' square and contains much for the eye to feast upon. Its colourful, lively design includes a Medusa head surrounded by four pairs of octagonal panels, some containing a stylised leaf, flower and a Solomon's knot. The overall design of this floor shows a lively, imaginative and artistic mind. The craftsmanship required for the laying out of this mosaic is disappointing as, in numerous places, the design is squeezed into a limited area. One example of this is that the north east chequer board is too large, so the framework of the adjacent panel is squeezed in and one line of its border has had to be omitted to take the design.

If we now look to the right we can see the 'Small Cross and Box' mosaic. This floor, in all probability, was crafted in the late 2nd century. The excavations in the 1960s detected some white tesserae on the southern side of the room underneath this later floor. The implications of this floor are interesting, suggesting that even in the late 2nd century the black and white geometric mosaics were still popular. The motifs on this floor are different to those in the 'Large Cross and Box' mosaic, in as much as some of the patterns are based on circles and are more varied. The white chalk tesserae are untidily laid compared to the neatness in this other room, which is a shame as this takes one's eye away from the imagination used for the crafting of the motifs.

Opposite the 'Greek Key and Medusa' mosaic are the remains of three black and white geometric mosaics rescued in 1987 from the back garden of a house which stands on the southern side of the West Wing. The third piece of mosaic to the right gives an insight into its design. The outer border consists of two lines of black tesserae, one line being five tesserae deep and the second line being two tesserae deep set in a white background. These lead the eye into the central design which is a combination of small and large black boxes contained in a white background. To the east, a small part of a black floral design can be seen. Also to be noticed are patches of blue/grey scorch marks – are these from the fire that destroyed the North Wing of the Palace around 270 AD?

If we now go east across the Lower Concourse to the next walkway we can view the 'Rectangles' mosaic. This floor could be seen as rather dull and boring, for as we view it, out of the corner of our eye we begin to notice the colourful creation in the room next door. Whether this room was a single room or part of a hall, I feel that the proprietor would not have paid money to have something created that had no impact. Perhaps, nearly two thousand years ago, this floor bore a symbolic message which would have been understood by all those ancient people who viewed or walked upon it. The overlapping rectangles, as we view them together, become more impacting to the eye and could symbolically stand for the coming together of cultures, ideas and/or beliefs. Thus, joined together, they become more vibrant, stronger and more noticed.

Just a few feet to the right is a room which contains the 'Floral' mosaic and the scar of the Palace discovery trench. The trench seems to have been cut for some distance before the digger driver stopped to see what was causing the mouth of the digger to work so hard. This was in April 1960 and Roman masonry, mosaic flooring and grey ware pottery had been brought to the surface. Consequently, in the Easter of 1961, trial trenches were dug in that same field for further investigation. This floral mosaic is vivid to the eyes with its variation of colours, coupled with a circular band showing rosettes alternating with leaves. In the north west corner dolphins can be seen facing towards a central vase. In the south east corner the dolphins are replaced by fish. In the remaining two corners the central vases have square-topped handles and the tendrils from the vases are longer and more exuberant than those in the south east and north west corners. It is a huge frustration that the central panel has been lost. The stones used for the tesserae were most colourful and the petals of the flowers and the leaves between them contain white chalk, red brick, yellow siltstone and a purple-toned Purbeck marble. Within the circular guilloche, red brick, blue Purbeck marble, grey limestone and a brownish/red sandstone can be seen. All of these colours are noticed in the spandrel designs. In my mind, I wonder why this polychrome mosaic is here when all around it the rooms contain geometric designs. Could it be that this floor is of a later date? Unfortunately, it contains no samian which would have helped to date it. This mosaic was lifted in 1961 and stored in a workroom for nearly six years before it was relaid exactly as it was found. The other thought that comes into my mind is that this mosaic was laid in homage to the mother Goddess deity. The clues are there, with the fish (feminine symbol of fertility) and the fish lived in water, a life giving element. The flowers live, grow and then die – although life is regenerated through their seeds. This mosaic is of unique quality and the skill required to construct this floor would be indistinguishable from those laid in Italy. For the Divine Mother a black and white mosaic would just not do!

The next room to review is named the 'Reverse Mosaic and Postholes', the smallest room in the North Wing. It is called the 'Reverse Mosaic' because the prominent colour is black with white pattern detail. This floor has escaped damage from the plough, although parts of it have sunk dramatically into the postholes of an earlier timber building, giving the mosaic a very distorted appearance. The design layout consists of alternate squares of red or blue framed within interlocking white lines. If we look to the south east corner, in the border of the dark grey, a white diamond can be seen. Is this the signature of the mosaicist? Interestingly, a single bright coloured tesserae of samian can be noticed in the red central panel. Is this just a repair or was it laid deliberately so the viewer would search for more samian and therefore view the floor for longer, and consequently digest and appreciate the work more? It seems that the red tesserae are a fine-grained fired clay and the blue a variety of Purbeck marble.

Next is Room 22. It seems that this floor has been a victim of the plough, only leaving a few patches of black and white which can be viewed today. What survives shows that there was a mosaic floor with a black design on a white ground, similar to the 'Rectangles' mosaic, the white tesserae being of chalk and the black/grey a silty shale.

The next room to view is Room 23. The floor in this room appears to have had a solid enough foundation to receive a mosaic. Although, perhaps over the course of time, the function of this room changed and the mosaic materials were lifted and perhaps stored and used elsewhere.

If we now make our way back towards the model of the Palace, using the walkway nearest to the north wall, just before the hypocaust we can view the 'Chequer and Stars' mosaic. The tesserae used in the construction of this floor are a hard, white chalk and a black silty shale. Part of this mosaic, the chequer pattern of alternating squares of black and white, can be viewed through the glass panel in the walkway. If we look to the south-east of this later floor we can see a white background with random stars of black tesserae. It could be that when the original floor in this room was removed, much of the original tesserae were re-used for this later mosaic.

CONCLUSION

Black and white mosaic floors have been known since the 2nd century BC and seem to have been the height of fashion in the 1st century AD. The North Wing of the Palace and the excavated parts of the West Wing are predominately black and white geometric designs. The only knowledge that we have regarding the mosaics in the South Wing was first recorded in 1805 when workmen digging the foundation of a house found a tessellated pavement about 13'6" in width and in the middle of this part of a base of a column was noted. The floor was composed of black and white tesserae. Unfortunately, the South Wing is buried underneath the A259 road and a number of houses. As for the East Wing, although tesserae were noted during the 1960s excavations, no mosaic or part of a mosaic was found in situ. It seems that the Palace would have been built by Mediterranean craftsmen, no doubt in a contemporary, Italian style. Some of the architecture within the Palace is similar to that found in the Domus Flavia, Domitian's Palace on the Palatine. The architect for the Domus Flavia was a man by the name of Rabirius; perhaps it is a possibility that Rabirius was the architect responsible for Fishbourne Roman Palace.

The Hyopcaust

The Nine Squared Mosaic

Chequerboard Mosaic

Shell Mosaic

Square and Diamond Pattern Mosaic

The Knot Mosaic

Rosette and Tessellated Floor

Large Cross and Box Mosaic

_Large Cross and Box Mosaic
showing the dividing wall_

Greek Key and Medusa Mosaic

Found under the Greek Key
and Medusa Mosaic

Mosaics from the West Wing

Small Cross and Box Mosaic

The Rectangles Mosaic

The Rectangles Mosaic

Mosaics from the West Wing

Floral Mosaic   *Room 22*

Floral Mosaic

Reverse Mosaic and Postholes

Chequer and Star Mosaic

Chapter IV

CUPID ON A DOLPHIN

1. The Modern Reading (Craftsmen and their Errors)
2. The Alternative Reading (Continuation of Life and Emotions)

THE MODERN READING

The sea horses of Neptune are said to have been constructed by a master mosaicist and an apprentice. We are told that the smaller sea horse could have been laid by the apprentice which may account for it looking undernourished and sickly.

Alternatively, we are told that the sea horses were constructed by two individual mosaicists not paying attention to each other's work. The larger sea horse is to the south side of the mosaic and the smaller one is on the north side. We are also told that the central motif, Cupid riding the dolphin, is laid off centre and to offset this mistake two pieces of foliage, beneath Cupid's left foot, are there to visually hide that error.

Two other mistakes are pointed out to us. The outer repeating triangles have a diamond on the north west, south west and south east corners, but on the north east corner one is missing. Also the border of continuing triangles changes direction in the north east corner – where the diamond is missing. One other error, not pointed out to us, is the width of two of the worm-like patterns surrounding the scallops in the south west corner. (This piece of work is useful for the interpretation of the second reading.) The guilloche patterning, we are told, acts as a framing device for the individual pictures within the mosaic.

This reading offers up the question as to why did the proprietor, who had the floor laid, not have these mistakes rectified? Well – perhaps he knew they were there for a reason. (This will be discussed in the Alternative Reading below.)

If we view some modern art, as well as appreciating the skill of the artist, we are sometimes offered a reading of what we are observing. Unfortunately, the craftsmen who laid this mosaic left little information about their work. It is possible that the ancient people who walked this mosaic knew how to interpret what was beneath their feet. Consequently, we are left with mythology, deities and superstitions as aids to reading this floor. They believed in good luck and bad luck. We know this, for at times boys were employed to make sure that guests entered certain rooms with their right foot first, for to enter by the left foot was deemed unlucky. Also they had a God called Janus who was the God of thresholds.

THE ALTERNATIVE READING

In mythology, sea horses are linked to the God Neptune. Neptune was the God given to freshwater springs providing drinking water – by societies who lived a distance from the sea. The larger sea horse could be read as being male and the smaller one as being female. Two things we could read from this – the continuation of the species through procreation, and for life to continue there is a need for fresh water.

The sea God Poseidon is represented here by the two sea panthers. One is male, as it has fangs; the other is female. Again, we have the theme of procreation of the species and, for life to continue, the availability of food from the sea. Water could have been in the four vases (cantharus), elaborately decorated, which would be showing respect to the water God, Neptune. The scallops motifs, set in the four corners of the mosaic, represent food from the sea. For food, as well as water, is needed for life to survive.

Please note how the vases are set just above the scallops, possibly providing a link between the importance of food and water needed to sustain life.

At this point of the reading, please note that the guilloche surrounding the motif of 'cupid on a dolphin' is larger and bolder than the guilloche around the sea horses, panthers and the scallops.

The motif of the 'cupid on a dolphin', set in the centre of this mosaic, is visually the most prominent piece of the floor and in antiquity cupids were often used symbolically to represent humans. Within this motif I feel that the cupid portrays a boy and the story unfolds as follows:

The boy was carried across the Bay of Naples, on the back of the dolphin, twice a day, so the boy could get to and from school. One day the boy fell ill and died. The dolphin, finding the boy dead on the beach, lay down next to him and also died.

Therefore, the central motif could be read as showing the emotions of friendship, devotion and love.

The final reading could be that the mosaic as a whole depicts the evolution of life, from the simple origins to the complications of emotions and relationships.

The ancient people believed in good and evil spirits (demons). We could perhaps interpret the guilloche surrounding the individual pictures, not just as a framing device, but intriguing traps for the inquisitive demons, in order to waylay the demon from contaminating the room. The 'mistakes' with the missing diamond (north east corner) and the changing direction of the triangle pattern on the outer design, would have been easy for the evil-one to notice.

The demon, now intrigued, now looks for more 'mistakes'. As he proceeds across the floor, the demon-traps become more subtle and harder to spot. He notices the two fatter, worm-like pieces of the guilloche on the outer pattern of the south west scallop design, and now, eagerly intrigued, looks at all the nine half-circle guilloche patterns which surrounds the scallops, sea horses and sea panthers for more errors. Now he approaches the central motif, the 'boy-cupid on a dolphin', but he is faced with a continuing circle of interlockingguilloche. Now his frustration is worked up to a frenzy as he cannot find the beginning or end of the guilloche. Suddenly he hears the approach of human footsteps and notices that dawn is breaking and flees the scene.

The two readings, though both different, still have one thing in common: neither can be proved right and neither can be proved wrong.

What I am suggesting in this chapter is that the proprietor of the palace, around 150 AD, by using the known images of mythology, decided to use these to tell his own story.

CUPID ON A DOLPHIN

Room 7

Southern Male

Northern Female

Panther Western Male

Panther Eastern Female

South East Corner

North East Corner

South West Corner (flawed)

North West Corner

Cupid on the Dolphin

Conclusion

At this moment in time, the Roman Palace rests peacefully, undisturbed and cared for, with affection, by the staff and volunteers under the protective umbrella of the Sussex Archaeological Society. But, what will the future hold for this iconic Roman building, the largest yet discovered north of the Alps? The major question being, will it once more be allowed to express itself with the help of more archaeological excavations? Excavations were drawn to a close after the summer of 2002, this being the first year of a proposed three year project design to understand the archaeology which is buried within the field to the east of the Palace's East Wing. Perhaps the most rewarding area for excavation, if indeed possible with such a high water-table, would be in the area south of the garden of the Palace's South Wing. Here, in the late 1960s, a canal was recognised running east from the deep-water channel. From within the silt layers of this old canal bed occupational material was excavated which included animal bones, quantities of pottery, leather and wooden objects. It seems today that the custodians of the Palace are the Sussex Archaeology Society and English Heritage, so where does responsibility lie, if indeed there is a responsibility to produce a project design for excavations in the future? Perhaps this joint responsibility has been diluted beyond recognition due to the lack of available finance. During the 1960s, Fishbourne Roman Palace was blessed with a benefactor – Ivan Margary; as well as having a healthy bank balance, this man harboured an active desire to understand more of this site's Roman past. At the back end of 2014, English Heritage archaeologists coordinated an excavation at Chedworth Roman Villa which brought to light a previously unknown mosaic floor. So, presumably, it seems that there is some available money to fund present day excavations. On this basis, I feel the time has come, for those people in authority within Sussex Archaeological Society, to engage with the spirit of Ivan Margary and to invite English Heritage archaeologists to an informal meeting at Fishbourne to discuss the possibility of drawing up, after thirteen years, a feasible project design to enlighten our knowledge and understanding of this site. BUT, of course I am well aware that there will be ripples and even waves of disapproval at this suggestion.